Copyright © 2023 by Nick Pernisco

All rights reserved.

No portion of this book may be reproduced in any form without written permission from the publisher or author, except as permitted by U.S. copyright law.

Awaken Your Inner Warrior

Awaken Your Inner Warrior:

Developing the Mindset for Overcoming Life's Great Challenges

By Nick Pernisco

Table of Contents

TABLE OF CONTENTS — 6
PREFACE — 7
INTRODUCTION — 10
RAISON D'ÊTRE — 14
    MAKE YOUR *RAISON D'ÊTRE* CONCRETE — 19
A WARRIOR'S INTENTION — 21
THE WARRIOR'S JOURNEY — 26
QUALITIES OF A WARRIOR — 39
    CREATIVITY — 49
    COURAGE — 58
    PERSISTENCE — 66
    RESILIENCE — 76
    DETERMINATION — 83
    ADAPTIVE — 89
    FOCUSED — 97
    AWARENESS — 107
    DISCIPLINED — 118
    INDIVIDUALISTIC — 125
    OPTIMISM — 137
CONCLUSION — 141
    THE QUALITIES OF A WARRIOR — 143

Preface

Welcome to Awaken Your Inner Warrior! A Journey of 1,000 miles begins with the first step, and you have taken that first step by picking up and reading this book. Before we begin, I want to tell you a little bit about my own story and why I believe that everyone should awaken their inner Warrior.

I was a professor in academia in 2011, when I was diagnosed with Parkinson's disease at the age of 33. I was caught completely off guard, since this was a disease that typically affected much older people. I wasn't ready to end my life's Journey yet, and the diagnosis sent me into a tailspin of depression and hopelessness. I could not understand why this was happening to me. I did not want a shorter life or progressively worse symptoms.

In 2015, I was in a very bad place, and I felt I had hit rock bottom. Then, it was a simple decision – either let the disease overtake me and let it kill me or step up and fight back. In 2016 I made the decision to fight back. I developed my brain to endure the hardships presented before me by studying ancient texts on war such as The

Art of War by Sun Tzu and The Prince by Machiavelli. The lessons I learned were unimaginable.

To my surprise, treating my illness like an enemy that deserved no mercy changed my life. I was suddenly able to endure the challenges brought to me, and I developed a Warrior Mindset, which put me directly at odds with my disease. In 2018, I underwent brain surgery to alleviate the symptoms of Parkinson's disease. I entered a surgery that most people fear by making jokes and laughing all the way to the operating room. This surgery has served me well, but it was no cure, and I continue to fight daily to maintain my positivity and keep up with my routines.

Since surgery, I have written several books about becoming a Warrior with Parkinson's, but I realized that the techniques and teachings of being a Parkinson's Warrior could be expanded and then distilled into knowledge that anyone can use to become a Warrior in their lives, no matter their situation or circumstances.

I realized that at some point in every person's life, they must develop a Warrior Mindset. Sometimes it is to get through a difficult time for them – perhaps they have an illness, or perhaps a family member does, or perhaps they are trying to get through school or a training that will lead to a better job and a better life, or maybe they want to start a company that will change the world, or run for office, or any number of other plans that require strength and resolve in order to "survive" and thrive.

My education from ancient texts served me well, and I have been able to modernize the main ideas and distill the philosophies into usable, tested strategies and tactics for developing the Warrior Mindset. What I present to you here are not those ancient texts, but my interpretation and perspective that has helped me so much. What you have here in your hands is a compendium of lessons learned and distilled in an easy-to-read format that you can digest in a day or so.

There is no correct way to read this book, and you may jump ahead at any time. However, the way I have found the material to be the most useful is to start at the beginning and continue straight to the end. You will want to read the book over and over throughout the years, so be sure to keep a copy by your bed stand.

So, let us take the second step in our Journey of 1,000 miles and begin learning the many qualities that will awaken your inner Warrior.

Introduction

Welcome to the beginning of your Journey to awaken your inner Warrior by developing the Warrior Mindset. Most of the time we can get by with just our natural, intuitive mindset. After all, we were created and then evolved to use our reflexes; if we find ourselves in a difficult situation, we can stay and 'fight' or we can leave and take 'flight.' This automatic body response has helped save our species over the millennia. If you have something to fear or an obstacle you must face, these innate reflexes act to help us overcome the situation and stay alive.

However, and for a multitude of reasons, many people feel they need great strength to overcome some of life's greatest obstacles. Some challenges are temporary, as when someone is studying in college and needs to pass that one difficult class, while other challenges are to be battled for an entire lifetime, as when someone needs to battle daily against an incurable disease. No challenge is the same, but all can be overcome in a sense. By developing a Warrior Mindset, you can have less worry and anxiety about the future and less despair and regret about the past, leaving you as the would-be Warrior to tend to the present.

As you read on, you will discover that most people wanting to develop the Warrior Mindset do so for their *raison d'être* – a fancy French phrase meaning **reason to be** or **reason for being**. You will discover that your reason is some*thing*, or most of the time, some*one* in your life. A businessperson wants to change the world for millions of people. A politician wants to improve their community. A person with an illness wants to spend as much time with their loved ones that they can. A father wants to be the best parent to his children. A student wants to pass their classes to hold a steady job and support a household. A marathon runner wants to challenge themselves to be their best, or perhaps to raise awareness and money for a cause that is important to them. We rarely do what's difficult for things, especially material things that come and go in our lives easily. Most of the things we do in life is to strengthen our relationships or in the service of others.

After you discover your *raison d'être*, you will learn the many essential qualities of a Warrior, and you will be on your way to developing a Warrior Mindset and overcoming, or at least able to confront, the largest challenges in your life. Interwoven in the essential qualities are lessons from history, as well as stories from more recent times. We will learn about the Warrior qualities of actual Warriors like the Spartans, as well as those of peaceful Warriors like Mahatma Ghandi and Martin Luther King Jr. We will also learn about regular everyday people who overcame addiction, illness, and all the challenges we each face in life.

As you read, you will also follow the fictional story of a great warrior, one who came from humble beginnings, but who rose to save their village when no one else could. Their struggle was of epic proportions, with disaster, failure, and even death around every corner, but they were still able to survive and return home with what they needed for their village. This story is an old story – only the names and places have changed. If you have read ancient mythology, you will find the Greeks and Romans had this same story. Even the *Bible* is filled with the same stories that we will read here. This mythology is so widespread and so ancient, that it was enshrined in modern literature with the release of the book, *The Hero with a Thousand Faces,* by the author, Joseph Campbell.

The various chapters in this book contain many stories, including some from my own life. I am not shy, and I will readily share serious stories like when I was prepared to die in order to have some relief from the pain of Parkinson's, and much lighter stories, such as my attempt to become a top-1,000 world-ranked pinball player. Both have lessons for us to learn from, and both have relatable bits that anyone can understand and empathize with. They also demonstrate that I have been on the path you are now on. I have been there – starting the 1,000-mile journey – and living to tell the tale. I hope to impart these tiny bits of wisdom upon you.

A word of warning, one which I will repeat later in this book: the 1,000-mile journey to becoming a Warrior, and developing a Warrior Mindset, do not guarantee success. You can become the ultimate Warrior, following every piece of advice, as well as embodying every quality of a Warrior, and still fail. Paradoxically, to become a Warrior, you must be willing to never give up, even if other minds would believe that failure is inevitable. You can want to be the richest person in the world, or the number one player in your sport, but the odds may be against you. This does not mean you should not try. This does not mean you should not believe. The Warrior tries and tries again, defeat only coming in death. Okay, perhaps that's a bit too dramatic. But the point remains. You must believe you will be successful even if you are likely to be defeated. To do so, you must remember your *raison d'être*.

Raison d'être

Originally a French word from the 14th century, no phrase better sums up this concept, with the literal (English) meaning *reason to be* or *reason for being*. This concept is an often-overlooked aspect to developing a Warrior Mindset, however, it is central to the idea behind developing a Warrior Mindset, and is, in fact, all encompassing. Let us examine more closely why everything we discuss in this book returns to your *raison d'être* – pronounced like English's *raisin*, but with an *on* instead of *in*, and then followed by the word *detra*. *Raision detra* – *raison d'être*.

Your *raison d'être* is the reason you are alive. It is the reason you want to continue living. To put a finer point on it, it is the reason you want to become a Warrior. The ancient Warriors of Sparta, who battled as a group of

300 soldiers in 480 B.C.E. in the Battle of Thermopylae, fictionalized in the film *300 (2006),* believed in fighting and winning, not just for themselves, but for their families, for their children, for their tribe and traditions. They faced 300,000 soldiers in an opposing force, and most died for their beliefs. You might ask, why not just give up in such situations? For the Spartans, surrendering would have meant succumbing to the enemy, and being derelict of their patriotic duty to defend their land and culture. Did they know their fight was futile? Perhaps. Did they know they must fight regardless of the outcome? Absolutely.

    This is only one example of Warriors who fought for their *raison d'être*. Many others exist in history, and not all are war related. For some, the fight might be against an illness, and their *raison d'être* is being with their family just a little longer. For others the fight might be a new business, and their *raison d'être* might be to change the world. For a student, their *raison d'être* may be to get good grades, graduate, and get a good job to support their family. For a soldier, their *raison d'être* may be to fight for the values of their country, and for the safety of its people. We all have a *raison d'être*, and for each of us it is unique.

Your *raison d'être* should not be confused with your so-called *purpose in life*. Having a purpose in life implies religion, fate, the universe starting and ending, and the belief that you are somehow special. I can tell you right now, *you are not special*. No one is. We all get up in the morning, do our thing during the day, have dinner, and go to sleep, all to do it over again. But in this truth lies the beauty of your *raison d'être*. It does not require you to be special. You can be a regular person and become a Warrior. You can be an absolute nobody, in fact, and pick yourself up and become a Warrior. I have met Warriors of all walks of life, ill patients, drug addicts, people in prison, all of whom wanted to become Warriors for their *raison d'être*. They overcame their obstacles because they realized they were not special, and they had to put in the work. No one is ready to make you a Warrior. You are not owed anything. You must choose to make the Journey yourself.

In this book, I will go into detail on the many qualities of a Warrior, and tie each of them back to the *raison d'être*. Because without a reason to be, to exist, there is no point in fighting, especially when the fight may take its ultimate toll emotionally and physically. After all, if you are a Warrior because you want to beat an illness, even an incurable one (by keeping it at bay), it may take every fiber of your being to get up in the morning and have the courage to go on with life. That is made easier when your *raison d'être* is your family, who loves you no matter what condition you are in, but for whom you want to be at your best.

The same goes for anyone starting a business. Money may be your goal, but will money be enough when you are six months in, working 80 hours per week, earning less than you did at your old job? If you wish to hold high office in your city or state, you will be attacked from every side, your name dragged through the mud at every turn. Having power is helpful if you want to do good things with it, but not if you just want the power for the sake of having power. In these situations, you will need a much more important reason to be.

For many, their *raison d'être* will likely be people, or some person in their life. As humans, we tend to do things for others, whether it be for someone's love, for someone's attention, or for our love of someone. In the end, you will likely notice that your *raison d'être* will be someone in your life you feel responsible for, or perhaps they are responsible for you in some way. Not all raisons d'être are for people, but you will notice as you go along your Journey to awaken your inner Warrior, your relationships and your bonds with others, will be what keep you going, even when all hope is lost. Since we need to push through that point of hopelessness, your *raison d'être* must be strong.

For some, changing the world is a very powerful *raison d'être*. If we look at the story of Mahatma Ghandi in India, he founded a movement and liberated his nation of British rule. He had all the qualities of a Warrior and was willing to make the sacrifices necessary to reach his goal. He ultimately paid with his life, but he is remembered to this day as the *Father of India*. In this case, Ghandi had an extreme focus on his goal, and his *raison d'être* was the people of India. Along his Warrior Journey, he gained fame, power, and a loving public. These were simply side effects to the work he put into his Journey. This is also true for people like Steve Jobs, whose company Apple invented the iPhone. His *raison d'être* was to change the world through technology, and he suffered emotionally at every difficulty on the Journey. Some say he was a difficult boss to work for, but this is only because he cared about doing things that others had not done. How do you have such a clear vision of the future and convey that idea to others? It is nearly impossible.

Remember, Ghandi and Jobs were not special in any way. Ghandi grew up in a small town in India but was later educated in London and took risks along his Journey. He was beaten and went on hunger strikes, all which made him grow even stronger. Jobs was born in San Francisco and then put up for adoption. Despite his hardships, early on he saw business as a chess board, and he could see several moves ahead of his rivals, which he used along his Journey to become stronger.

Make your *raison d'être* concrete

Now, think about *your* reason to become a Warrior. Examine the challenges in your life. List them all on a piece of paper. Make sure they are your biggest challenges. Now think about what these challenges have in common. Now merge those challenges into a single challenge. Make it into a verb. It can be concrete. TO stop smoking. TO get well. TO graduate. TO sell a million units. It can also be abstract. TO be stronger. TO win more. TO be happy. TO make my parents proud.

Now think about *why* you want to overcome this challenge. How do you benefit? How do those around you benefit? Be truthful with yourself. Reach deep within you and pull out the real reason. Remember, your *raison d'être* is often, but not always, a person. If you want to change your own life for yourself, then you are the *raison d'être*. Be sure that your *why* is positive – we cannot sustain a negative *raison d'être* for long for it will destroy us. Revenge is not a valid *raison d'être*. Violence is not valid either. Be positive, think long term, and decide on your *why*. The *why* is your *raison d'être*.

Now, your challenge and your *raison d'être* are forever linked. Write them down as we do below. Write your challenge as a verb, followed by your *raison d'être* as a verb. Be as specific or as vague as you prefer. For example:

TO stop smoking TO live longer for my kids.
TO live my best life TO enjoy life with my family.
TO start a business TO change the world.
TO be stronger TO be taken seriously.

Congratulations. This is your *mantra,* your challenge, or whatever you want to call it. Print it out, tattoo it on your arm, do what it takes to make this a part of your being. Start each day by looking in the mirror and reciting it and end each day by looking in the same mirror and repeating it again.

Your mantra is what will transform you into a Warrior. It is why you are on this Journey. It is why you will forsake so much in your life to achieve this. It will not be easy. There will be a lot of sacrifices in your future. But if you know WHY you are doing what you *want* to do – what you *need* to do – you are one step closer to achieving it.

You are ready for the next step: learn the qualities of a Warrior.

A Warrior's Intention

Before we explore the qualities of a Warrior, we must discuss the Warrior's Intention. With the Warrior's Intention, you have made the decision to dedicate yourself – and even your entire life – to the achievement or overcoming of something challenging. This is an important intent, and you should be proud of even considering undertaking such a challenge. However, it is important to understand that you are setting this intent yourself, and this intent will carry its energy into the world, and from that moment, you no longer have control of that intent. You have the power to become a Warrior, but you cannot control who or what you will face in your path.

Said more plainly, you can control the actions you take in the world, but you cannot control the actions of others.

Becoming a Warrior does not make you a master of the universe, only a master of yourself. This book is not intended as a manual for overcoming the force of another person or of a given situation, but to prepare you for that battle. There may be times that you will want to have your way, just by willing it to be, but this attitude only leads to the Warrior's eventual downfall. There will be further discussion about this later in the book, but it must be made clear from the beginning: you cannot master others, only yourself. Often, this is enough to overcome nearly any challenge.

The Warrior's Mindset can therefore be used to help you overcome any internal struggle. These are struggles that come from your own deficiencies, typically derived from weakness of will. The Warrior Mindset helps strengthen your resolve and helps eliminate weaknesses.

If you resolve to do something that has been possible for others but not for you, this is where the Warrior Mindset will help you in your Journey. Imagine such challenges as reducing debt, becoming healthier, or graduating from school – these are battles of internal will that the Warrior Mindset is perfectly suited for.

However, if your goal is to develop a Warrior Mindset to overcome a challenge with external forces, then you must fight knowing the ultimate result may be out of your hands. Several examples of this include overcoming an incurable illness, battling against an attacking force, or earning the love or respect of another person – these are battles in which the Warrior must battle with external, and often opposing, force that affects the ultimate outcome.

Does this mean one battle is worth fighting than another? Not at all. If your will is good, and your mantra is positive, then developing a Warrior Mindset will be valuable and should be undertaken. This is not meant to discourage you from developing a Warrior Mindset and overcoming your specific challenge, but to make you aware of your own limitation – you only have control of yourself. This is not to say you cannot use a Warrior's savvy to help force a favorable outcome with an external challenge or challenger, but you do not have complete control of most situations. As a Warrior, you control your own actions and your mind, but you do not control any external factors outside of yourself.

To further explain this using an example from history, we can look no further than the example given to us by one of America's greatest presidents, Abraham Lincoln. When Lincoln was just starting out in politics, he had to make a name for himself and start small. He decided he could use his skills most beneficially in the Illinois state house, so in March 1832 he ran for an Illinois state house seat. In August of that year, he lost that race. Even though he was discouraged, Lincoln was right on schedule for Campbell's book about mythical heroes. Lincoln was a self-taught lawyer with a successful practice, so he used this to refine himself and make connections that would help him later on. Lincoln said he would continue running until he won, and so in 1834 he ran again for another Illinois state house seat. This time he won. In eight more years he would be a US Representative from Illinois, and in a few more he would become a US Senator. In 1860 he ran for and won the US presidency.

None of this would have been possible without his Warrior Mindset. Even though he was strong, he faced many external challenges – by opponents, by people who did not like him, and by his own party. When he decided to begin his Journey, Lincoln knew he would confront these forces outside of himself, and of which he had not control. But with perseverance and dedication, he eventually went on to become America's 16th president during a time in American history that needed someone like him to re-unite the country.

    I personally know of many people with incurable diseases like Parkinson's disease who have developed the Warrior Mindset to hold off their incrementally worsening of symptoms. They understand that the disease is progressive, and no matter what they do they will become worse over time. They also know there is no cure to the disease, but that has not stopped them from deciding to battle. Despite the obstacles in their way, they have decided to fight the disease every day by not giving in to the inevitable. They eat well, they exercise daily, and they practice mindfulness for the mind, body, and soul. They have taken control of the aspects of their lives they can control – their positive attitude and their perseverance.

However, they know the disease is a brutal opponent, and no matter what they do they are destined to progress in their illness. But they know that their life would be a lot worse if not for their Warrior Mindset.

The most important take away from this section is that you are only in control of your own thoughts and actions. Life, as with every important challenge we face, is full of forces counteracting our best efforts to come out ahead. While some challenges only come from within as internal struggles, other challenges bring external struggles, which we must meet and counteract with our own challenges. This knowledge is not to discourage you, but to strengthen you to battle through an opposing force. Become a Warrior and strengthen yourself for the battle.

The Warrior's Journey

The Warrior's Journey is an adventure the Warrior embarks on when they accept the responsibility of becoming a Warrior. The following is the story of a Warrior, and while it is fiction, it details the Journey made by the millions who came before. Join in reading the Warrior's Tale and relate your own struggles and challenges to this Warrior's. This Warrior can be anyone, but for this story, our hero goes by the she/her pronouns.

The Warrior's tale.

Once, long ago, far away, there was a person – the hero of our story – who wanted to change her world dearly. Her entire family lived in a small village stricken with drought, poverty, and which was constantly besieged by an onslaught of invaders. While the young men and women of the village were dying in the battlefield, the older generation was dying of diseases never seen before. The children were too hungry to think, so learning became difficult for the new generation. The entire village would be wiped out in a matter of years, if not sooner.

One day, a mage came to visit and offered to help the village. The mage needed one person to lead the village, and because of her desire to help her fellow villager, our hero was the only one who could do it. The mage reached out to her and said, *you must come with me if you want your village to survive.* Our hero did not want to leave her village, at least not while the village was in so much trouble. She felt her skills and abilities were best utilized at home.

Our hero declined the challenge because of her commitment to the people of the village. No doubt, the status quo also felt the most comfortable. Even plagues, war, and famine seemed better than what could be awaiting our hero out there in the world. Our hero was disappointed, in herself, and for the village. Here was her moment to stand up and save the village, and she was too afraid to take up the challenge.

Overnight there was a huge infestation of wasps. The wasps made the land unable to support the growth of new crops, making the food in the stores the last of all time. The soldiers found it difficult to fight the onslaught of invading armies because the wasps were flying everywhere. Half the army was lost. The hero's parents came out to swat the wasps and pray for them to go away, and they were consumed by the wasps. They gave their lives for the village. Our hero had nothing left. Now it was only a matter of a season or two before the town would fall. This was the worst thing to ever happen to her.

The next day, the mage was saddling up his horse and preparing to leave. Our hero appeared and told the mage the story about the food, the soldiers, and her parents. She had nothing left to lose and she wanted to go with him to find help for the village. The mage realized our hero was desperate, and that she was now considering going with the mage for the wrong reasons. After all, the hero had already refused the call to adventure due to a lack of courage.

The mage said to the hero, "I'm afraid there is a storm brewing, and you will not withstand it." The hero considered everything that was lost overnight, and how much more would be lost if she did not seek help. She stood up straight with her hands made into fists and she replied, "I am the storm."

The mage agreed to help our hero.

Upon leaving the town through the gates, our hero was already faced with challenges. There was only one animal in town capable of carrying supplies, a mule, which did not want a human on its back. How would our hero make it through the various terrain necessary to reach help if this animal would not carry her? The mage was patient, and would wait for our hero, even if she was slow. Knowing this, our hero transferred all the satchels on her person to the mule. The mule was already loaded with supplies but didn't mind the extra weight if the cargo was not human. This freed our hero to walk unencumbered beside the donkey, helping her increase her speed and saving her strength. Our hero displayed great *creativity*.

After a day of travel, the mage told our hero that she would need to enter the sacred cave. In this cave, the mage said our hero would face a great challenge. In fact, she would face demons from her past, but she must overcome these demons to drink from the cave well. Our hero felt more afraid than she had ever felt, but she slowly entered the cave. After a moment she spotted the well. She went straight for it but was suddenly confronted by millions of wasps and rabid bats flying toward her, but she continued walking. Next, she was confronted by enemy soldiers. She only needed to strike these giants to be rid of them. Finally, she reached the well. Before she was able to scoop some water from the well, she looked inside and saw herself dying. She didn't know how she was dying but she looked about 10 or 20 years older than she was at the time. She finally drank a handful of water and was suddenly transported back to the mage and the mule. She was afraid of what she would find, but she knew that *courage* is always accompanied by fear.

Our hero continued through the desert. As she walked, the mage kept reminding her of the reasons she was undertaking this Journey. It was for her family, her village, for peace, for everything she had ever known. After walking for 10 days, our hero reached a town gate. The wind and flying sand made it difficult to make out the name of the town. But she soon realized that she was back at the beginning of her Journey, at the gates of her own town. The mage simply told our hero that she must continue forward. So, she did just that. She kept walking through the desert, and every 10 days she would arrive back at the beginning of her Journey. This had happened five times when our hero was about to give up. Then she thought to herself, *once more.* After the sixth try, she reached a signpost that showed her town on one side, and the word *Redemption* on the other. She hadn't seen this sign before, but she felt something was different this time. It was only due to her **persistence** that she had made it this far.

After more than 100 days on her walk across the desert, she was out of water, she was exhausted, and the mule keeled over and died. She had, at best, two days of supplies left. She asked the mage for help, but he could not offer any – only advice about the Journey itself. She thought this was it. It was over. She had a good run, but she had reached the end of her line. With her tired body half entrenched in the sand, she asked the mage how much longer until she could resupply. The mage told her the oasis was right in front of her — about 100 meters away. She only needed to crawl a bit more. So, our hero mustered every cell in her body and crawled the 100 meters. She was so tired that it took her over two hours to reach the oasis. She reached the top of a dune and saw the oasis below. It was filled with water, next to shade, and with animals grazing and drinking. Our hero used her last bit of strength to roll herself down the dune, finally making a splash into the water below. Because of her **resilience**, our hero was able to rest, recover, reload water and food. She even found a camel to carry her and all of the supplies.

    Our hero spoke with the mage, asking how much longer until the end of the Journey. She was of course concerned about bringing help back to her village, but her resolve and **determination** were never in doubt. She told the mage that she would succeed, at whatever cost to herself, to help her people. The mage said that they were only a tenth of the way to their destination. Our hero could not believe that after so many days walking through the desert, they had ninety percent of the Journey still ahead of them. Our hero stood at the edge of the oasis, made a power pose in which she outstretched her arms, and then let out a primal scream. *"Ahhhhhhhhh!"* The mage stared at her, with a slight fear in his gaze. She yelled out to the mage from across the oasis and said simply, "Let's do this."

Our hero, along with the mage and their new camel, continued their Journey. Along the way, things did not go to plan all the time. In fact, there was no real plan, except to reach the help the mage had promised. At one point, they encountered a large bridge over a huge expanse of water. Crossing it, with the wind hitting her face and swaying the bridge, seemed nearly impossible. So, our hero rode the camel down to the water and crossed the expanse atop the camel, avoiding the bridge all together. Another time, the desert seemed to stop – an invisible barrier? Or something else? So, our hero changed direction until the end of the barrier, going around it, but going 25 kilometers out of the way from the original direction. Our hero knew she had to ***adapt*** when the situation called for it.

At one point during the Journey, our hero and her party reached a small town. This was not the destination, but the small town did have many things that could be valuable to our hero. They had weapons, enough to beat her village's enemies. They had street vendors who could deliver fresh fruits and vegetables daily to her town. There were many other mages who offered to help for a price. This seemed like the destination, or if at minimum, *a destination*. The mage told our hero that some of what she needed was here at this village. But nothing at this village would bring her own town the resources it needed to become self-sufficient. This demonstrated out hero's **awareness** of everything going on around her. So, our hero bought herself a few fresh fruits, and she continued on her way, following the mage to continue the search for his solution.

After ten more days of walking, our hero could feel she was still far from the end of the Journey. Her mood had changed, and the mage could feel it as well. She was upset, would cry occasionally and suddenly, and was very silent for a time. They reached a giant cliff overlooking an ocean. The mage said, "this is where we turn North." As the mage began to turn, our hero stayed at the cliff and sat down. She was aware of her feelings, and how it was affecting not only her but the mage and even the camel as well. Our hero closed her eyes and meditated. She cleared her mind of everything and ***focused*** on her breath and on the fresh air coming from the ocean. In doing so, she eliminated all mental distractions from her mind. It was night by the time she opened her eyes again. The mage had already set up camp for the night. Our hero visited the mage in his tent and apologized for her mood. The mage said there was no need to apologize, and that it would be alright to give up now. Our hero had just cleared her head and said that they would continue forward in the morning.

    More time had passed, and our hero's body was aching, but she continued forward. Sensing that the end of the Journey was near, she found that her daily routine helped keep her motivated and ready for anything the desert had in store. She woke up at sunrise, meditated for 30 minutes, ate food and drank water from her supplies, and attended to the camel. Her and the mage walked each day from mid-morning until the sun would be near its setting, and then set up camp. All to do this again the next day. This ***discipline*** kept her focused on her goal and put her control of the world, rather than the other way around.

Finally, after so long, our hero could see a large castle made of gold in the distance. The mage said that they were nearing the end of their Journey. When they reached the gates of the castle, the mage told our hero that he could no longer help her from then on. She must complete the remainder of the Journey alone. On her own, our hero used her *individualism* to confront the greatest moment of her life with her own abilities. She slowly made her way past the gates and into the castle courtyard. The inside of the castle was like an entire city, with all the weaponry, food, and natural resources her town could ever need. She was greeted by the leader of the castle city, the Queen.

The Queen asked about our hero and listened to her story. Our hero used her cunning to convince the Queen that she herself was a powerful queen, with her own army and her own resources. She left out the important part about how her town was besieged by an enemy. The Queen, in her wisdom, knew our hero would not be there alone if not out of desperation. The Queen discussed her own problems with an opposing kingdom, a kingdom that both the Queen and our hero had problems with. Our hero, **optimistic** that she would succeed in her Journey, finally disclosed the truth — about the besieging army, about the plagues, and about the wasted land. Our hero proposed an alliance. The Queen would help her fellow queen and when her town was back on its feet, it would provide resources to the Queen. They would share soldiers, food, and resources to conquer their common enemy. The Queen agreed.

With that action, our hero had herself become a Queen. Perhaps a selfish and **individualistic** move, but she did it out of necessity for her people's safety and security. Our hero was given safe passage back to her own village, which turned out to be only a half day's walk away from her new ally. The mage had set up this Journey to test our hero, and she of course passed. Upon returning to her village, she told the villagers about her Journey and what she had secured for the village. Everyone rejoiced and chanted *Long live the Queen!* The new Queen knew that she could have failed in her Journey, but she possessed all the qualities of a Warrior, and the universe had been in her favor this time, so she did succeed. And she ruled for the rest of her life, which was longer than what she had seen in the cave well. Her people flourished, and intermixed with the Queen of the Golden Castle, making their bonds even stronger.

Qualities of a Warrior

A Warrior can have many qualities that can take any number of shapes. Whenever we think of someone as a Warrior, we might conjure up images of ancient Samurai warriors or modern-day military officers. The fact is these types of warriors have great physical and mental strength, and they are often engaged in war tactics. However, when we talk about Warriors here in this book, we want to focus on Warriors who use their mental strength to overcome internal obstacles rather than external threats of war. In this respect, Warriors as we discuss them here do not require great physical strength. The Warriors we discuss here do not even require winning or losing, as sides often do in war. As such, our Warrior is not interested in the zero-sum game, where there must be a winner and a loser. Perhaps a winner-takes-all scenario is necessary for your *raison d'être*, but this is rare.

The truth is anyone can decide to go on the Warrior's Journey and act in accordance with the qualities of a Warrior. As long as your success is not mired in superlatives (I want to be the best, I want to live the longest, I want to make the most money), then the

Warrior's Journey is open to everyone. See, to become a Warrior you need to recognize that you are not fighting an external battle with someone else, but an internal battle with yourself. Even if your challenge is to take on an opposing force, the battle is always inside of you. Let us examine the change of mindset that exists in a Warrior. First, you must change your superlatives: "I want to be MY best," "I want to live the longest I CAN," "I want to make the most money I CAN make." You have just changed the responsibility from the world giving you something, to you being responsible for your own Journey. With this change alone, you are beginning to change your Mindset. There is only one richest person alive, imagine if there were eight billion of them? It is not possible. The hero makes their own path and pushes their own story forward.

    This is all to introduce you to the fact that your Warrior's Journey is about you. It is about what you want to get out of it and for your *raison d'être*. This book is meant to be self-help, not self-sabotage. The last thing I want to do is set you up for failure. It is far better to start with success in mind.

    There are ten main qualities that a person must master to Awaken their inner Warrior. Each is described here in brief, and later chapters we will further explore each one. When you read about each quality below, consider how each applies to your own Journey. Think back to the hero in our story and how she used each quality to overcome her challenges.

A Warrior must possess creativity.

Creativity is a skill or sense using our imaginations to problem solve. As children we were taught to be creative and told that creativity is a virtue. However, as we became older we became more set in our ways and our brains became more automatic in action and in thought. As adults we do not use our imaginations as much as we did as children. This is the reason that so many people stumble when faced with a difficult situation. Creativity allows us to solve problems in new and interesting ways and it also allows us to improvise solutions that may not be visible at first. Your life is not written. There is no definitive answer to any question about life. You will make mistakes when you use your mind in create ways. Ultimately, you decide the course of your life and the creativity you use to achieve your greatness.

A Warrior must possess courage.

Courage is not a quality you can simply claim – you cannot simply say *I'm courageous* – but rather it must be proven. Possessing courage means being afraid and still moving forward and through the situation. Someone who possesses courage is afraid – fear is necessary for courage to exist, for without fear there can be no courage. Possessing courage is not the same as learning to live with and manage fear, but quite the opposite. To possess courage, you must begin at point *A*, face your fear, and arrive at point *B*. Courage is a Journey, and it is one you must make on your own.

A Warrior must be persistent.

Persistence is the act of not giving up upon defeat. If you are persistent, you may still not succeed, this is a sad truth – nothing in life is guaranteed – but you cannot be successful without persistence. Every business owner, every great leader, every person who has done anything of great importance, whether it be defeating cancer or running for president, has faced great roadblocks, hurdles, and setbacks. No one would have blamed them for surrendering in the face of such odds. But persistence kept them fighting and lifting themselves again and again after defeat.

A Warrior must be resilient.

In a way, resilience and persistence are similar – both are about not giving up in the face of defeat. However, resilience is not about whether you bounce back in the face of obstacles, but rather about *how* you bounce back. Some people call this grit (putting in all your effort and then-some to complete a task or challenge), others call this stoicism (the mental ability to minimize swings between positive and negative emotions), but regardless of what you call it, resilience is about bouncing back with greater force at every setback or roadblock. It is about having an attitude that says *I will never surrender*. It is this attitude that will keep you fighting at your weakest moment.

A Warrior must possess determination.

Are you determined to succeed? Will you succeed? How you answer these two questions is reflective of your determination – the belief in yourself that you will succeed. If you go into a situation with doubts about your own ability or chances of success, you have already lost. You must be determined to succeed, and you must believe it. Will you succeed? *YES!* With any other answer, you are giving yourself permission to fail. "*I wasn't smart enough.*"

"I wasn't healthy enough." "I didn't have it in me from the beginning." These are all excuses that a Warrior never uses because a Warrior is determined to succeed, even if in the end they do not.

A Warrior must be adaptive.

The enemy moves left, you must move right. The enemy moves down, you must move up. When the enemy makes a move you have never seen before you must adapt. Being adaptive is changing tactics (the day-to-day or minute-to-minute activities) and even strategies (the bigger plan) midway through your Journey. You must be nimble and be ready to adapt as the situation unveils itself to you. You will face unexpected situations on your Journey that will knock you off course. A business associate leaves, a political opponent finds something to use against you, your illness worsens, you receive a failing grade on your exam. In all these situations, the Warrior's response is, *"this is unexpected. What's my next move?"* Life almost never goes to plan, and plans change over time, sometimes moment to moment. You must learn to adapt if you are to succeed.

A Warrior must be focused.

You have heard of the phrase, *Jack of all trades, master of none*. You are welcome to be a jack of all trades, but you will never achieve great successes if you do. Success in life requires strict focus on the object of your attention. If you are trying to achieve something incredible and that requires a Warrior Mindset, you must be focused. Losing focus leaks your energies (which are limited) on unnecessary exploits. You must let go of your million ideas in your brain and aim for one and one alone. An Olympic athlete will train every waking hour of the day and dream about their big moment at night. Focus is key and essential.

A Warrior must possess awareness.

Are you aware of your body's reaction to heat or cold? Can you tell when you are losing focus or becoming angry? How well do you know yourself? Awareness, especially self-awareness, is critical for a Warrior. Knowing your strengths and weaknesses, understanding your emotions, recognizing your effect on others – these are all keys of self-awareness. This awareness is sometimes called emotional intelligence – how in tune are you with the world? You must be aware of yourself as well as the situations around you for they could prove critical to your success. Having awareness and reacting appropriately to this awareness are essential qualities for becoming a Warrior.

A Warrior must possess discipline.

Discipline is doing what must be done even though you may or may not want to do it. For a Warrior, this means developing good routines and habits that contribute positively to your physical, emotional, or mental state. Many point to exercise and eating well as areas they are least disciplined in. Discipline is about creating processes that may be run and rerun on an ongoing basis. An Olympic athlete trains every day – it is a routine. A healthy person develops a routine that may involve waking up early, walking for an hour, meditating for 15 minutes, and eating a healthy breakfast each day. Developing a routine that works for you will make you stronger and make your goals more attainable. A positive routine leads to positive discipline.

A Warrior must be individualistic.

Most people find individualism a negative quality. However, for a Warrior it is essential. Recall the videos or demonstrations shown on flights that explain how to use the oxygen mask. The flight attendants tell you to put on your own mask before assisting your child or others. This is because you cannot help others unless you help yourself first. What good is giving your attention to someone else while you are sitting helplessly and gasping for air? You must learn to say *no* to unnecessary distractions. You must have the energy and singular effort to succeed in your plan. Saying *yes* to someone else's plan means saying *no* to yours. Remember we have limited energy and resources. Returning to our example about the airplane – after you have affixed your mask and that of your family, do you help everyone else on the plane, or do you secure yourself for the imminent hard landing?

A Warrior must be optimistic.

Optimism is the ability to look at life with hope, which is different from positivity, which is the ability to feel a positive emotion in the moment. You can feel positively or negatively about your current situation, but a Warrior chooses to look beyond the current moment and think optimistically about the future and what it will bring. Of all the qualities of a Warrior, optimism is the only one that must be actively chosen. You cannot become optimistic through practice – you must decide to be optimistic. When bad things happen, and they will, you must allow those things to simply slide off you. You must continue to believe that, even though today is not your day, tomorrow may be your day. You must keep believing that life is a series of adventures, not a series of obstacles to overcome.

A Warrior has many qualities that are specific to their given situation.

Although not listed here, some Warriors may need a few more qualities to help they through a particular situation. These qualities can be added on as needed once you have developed your Warrior Mindset. For example, it helps to be *positive* when battling an illness. It helps to be *ethical* if you are running for office. It helps to have *mental stamina* if you are a student. It helps to be *able to work with others* if you are a business or community leader. Some additional qualities are more obvious than others. However, the essential eleven characteristics we just highlighted will be the focus of this book.

You are now prepared for the transformation that lays ahead. Do not forget, you are on a Journey – life is a series of adventures – and you are about to continue yours. Read on to learn details about each of the qualities you must possess to succeed in your Warrior's Journey.

Creativity

During childhood, we were taught that creativity was a good thing. In school we were given positive feedback by teachers and by our parents for being creative. Whenever we would bring home some art piece we made with crayons or when we used paste to create a collage, our parents told us *good job* or gave us some other reward for being creative.

The problem with creativity arrived for most of us during high school. We were suddenly told a different story, that too much creativity was bad, and that we should pursue more serious hobbies and take much more serious attitudes towards life. For many of us, this killed the creative process we had begun in elementary or preschool. Fortunately, our creativity bubbled up when we had to write a short story for English or figure out how to solve a math problem we had never seen before.

This means that, luckily, creativity never left us and is in fact alive and well. The skills we used to create that artwork from first grade remains inside us to this day. In many professional fields such as management and law, those creative skills must be used to get ahead. Many fields that are not traditionally considered creative such as accounting and engineering require a lot of creative thinking. That is because creative thinking is the ability to contemplate a problem outside of the prescribed ways of thinking to arrive at a unique solution.

The field of mathematics provides us a great example of how creativity can be used to solve a problem. Without getting too much into math itself, think about algebra and how you need to sometimes find a creative way of arriving at the correct solution. Mathematics, at least how it is taught in school, uses creativity – with multiple pathways to arrive at the same correct answer.

Recently I was helping my niece with a math problem from school. She explained the problem to me, and I was quickly able to find the correct answer (it was not that difficult). My niece was upset at this. The problem was that the way math is taught in the 21st century in schools is much different than the way it was taught in the 20th century and before. This fact can be frustrating for grownups trying to help their kids with their homework. I can look at a problem and demonstrate how I arrived at a correct solution, but my niece said that this is not how the teacher taught it, and that she needed to use little boxes to demonstrate how she arrived at the correct answer.

One aspect of this exercise was enlightening; that there are at least two ways to arrive at the correct solution.

Creativity is an important skill for a Warrior. To attain the Warrior Mindset, we must practice creativity so that we can solve problems no one has solved before or to solve it better. There are some with the negative attitude who might say, *"why bother? Everything has already been invented/ Why reinvent the wheel?"* But a true Warrior can find new solutions to old problems. They are never satisfied with the status quo, with the way that things have always been done. As the phrase goes, *when there is a will, there is a way*. We could paraphrase that famous quote to adapt it for our purposes: *when there is a need, there is a solution waiting to solve it.*

In the 1860s, there did not exist a simple way to easily fasten two or more pages together and then release them without damage. There was an obvious need for people to do this in offices all around the world. At that point, when the need was large enough, someone invented the paperclip – a piece of wire originally invented for cleaners who wanted to fasten a ticket to a piece of clothing without harming it. The paperclip was so important, and the need for a good product so in demand, that within ten years, a new and improved style of paperclip had been invented. As office work grew and more paperwork was created (this was before computers and e-mail), the paperclip industry was in full swing – by 1900 there had been 50 varieties of paperclips patented. The paperclips we use today were being used in Britain in the 1870s and never patented. Each paperclip improved upon or found a novel way to address a problem with past versions. How is that for finding many solutions to a problem?

In the 1990s, General Motors realized there was a need in the market for an electric car. After years of research and development, they released the first commercially available electric car, the EV-1. They had found a need – people who wanted to drive an eco-friendly car – and they devised a way to satisfy that need. The car was so expensive to build that it was only leased out to people, so no one actually owned one. After a few years of trying to grow the market, the car was discontinued. There was still a problem needing to be solved. People still wanted eco-friendly cars that took no gasoline.

Enter Elon Musk, the billionaire entrepreneur who had made his riches first at Paypal. In 2004, he took an active role at Tesla, an electric car manufacturer named after the famous scientist who invented DC power. After years of trying to build his company, drawing early investors, using his own money, and being sued by traditional car manufacturers, in 2019, the Tesla model 3 became the best-selling luxury car in America. In 2020, Elon Musk was named the richest man on the planet. The surprise twist here is, in a case of irony, General Motors said in 2021 that its entire car lineup will be all electric by 2035.

Creativity is critical if you are to survive the twists and turns of life, let alone the specific challenges you are trying to overcome. Always know that there is more than one way to solve a problem, even a problem that appears to have only one solution. Getting to that solution in a way that no one else has in the past takes creativity. Discouragement can come from different people, even those closest to you. Do not let their negative attitudes dissuade you from finding your own solution in your own way.

Ways to be more creative.

Thus far, we have explored some abstract ideas about creativity. We have also focused on some specific stories that demonstrated how creativity helped people get through challenges. What follows are some concrete methods for practicing creativity and making sure your creative muscles are strong for when you need them.

Train the creativity muscle daily. This cannot be stressed enough. Just like every quality of a Warrior, creativity is a muscle that must be nurtured to grow and be available when we need it. Use every opportunity to practice creativity by doing something creative every day. Remember that creativity can exist even if there is one known answer to a question or challenge. The Warrior Mindset means finding the paths not taken by others to reach a goal of some sort.

A great exercise you can use to challenge your creativity daily involves solving puzzles. Crossword puzzles, word games, and even sudoku can teach us to be strategic and to use our creativity to overcome challenging situations. Using the example of playing crossword puzzles, consider that there is only one correct answer for each clue, but if you are having difficulty solving the *down* word, try solving any of the *across* words to help you build the *down* word. In real life, we call this solving by deduction – knowing the answer to *A* helps us arrive to the answer of *B*. Sudoku is another casual game that can help us train our creativity and which uses deduction. Just like with crossword puzzles, there is only one answer per square, but knowing the numbers in particular squares will help in finding undiscovered numbers in adjacent rows and columns.

Look for different perspectives. Another way to be creative is to explore other perspectives – on life, on your work, on relationships – there are many ways of looking at life and there is no one way of doing things. You may find it enjoyable to read the biographies of historical people who have had to overcome similar challenges, and you will likely discover the use of creativity in ways you had previously not thought of. In the same vein, find a contemporary peer who can help guide you and offer creative ways to overcome the challenges you are facing. In many cases, there is no point in reinventing the wheel, and a creative solution that someone else used may be adapted to your own situation. This is a case of *"the more you know, the more you know."* New learning scaffolds and builds upon past learning.

While it may be difficult to ignore criticism from people closest to you, never change your perspective to one of negativity. If you are to attain a Warrior Mindset, being influenced by negative voices that say *it cannot be done* should be ignored. While there may be valid reasons to not attempt finding a solution to a particular problem, these reasons should come from you, not from negative voices that only influence you to fail. Creativity is a strange thing – no one in history has created something new or done anything novel or interesting without breaking the status quo. However, the status quo is the only thing people know until it is replaced by something new. Just remember the story about the paperclips!

Never stop learning. The best thing you can do to train your creative muscles is to never stop learning. This does not mean you should go back to school and start a new degree program. Instead, you should approach life, and all that happens in it, as a new learning opportunity. Read books, biographies and otherwise, to learn how others have lived their lives. Travel the world and learn about other cultures. You will learn how these humans, who are just like you, took the earth's resources, just as your culture has, and made something unique and important. Be the most knowledgeable person of your corner of the world. Be sure that whatever you do, you are the best and have the most knowledge of it. Remember, new knowledge builds on existing knowledge. *The more you know, the more you know.*

I have had the opportunity to travel around the world, and the most eye-opening places for me were Delhi, India, and Amsterdam, The Netherlands. In both places, I had the opportunity to see how different people approach life, healthcare, getting around town, dealing with other people, doing business, and much more. The experiences opened my eyes to how we as humans are all the same, but how culture makes us act differently. The way of life in both places was much different than the way of life back in the United States, and with these new experiences I received the gift of knowledge. This gift of knowledge, even on some short trips, changed my perspective enough to affect my actions the next time I faced a creative challenge.

Creativity is an evolutional gift that we have and that the rest of the animal kingdom does not (generally speaking – there are many species that exhibit some degree of creativity). To become true Warriors, we must learn to use our creativity to find solutions to problems that seem unsolvable at first. If there is a solution, you must be inclined to find it, even when it seems impossible. This is the mark of someone with the Warrior Mindset.

Courage

Courage is an essential trait for any Warrior. What exactly is courage, and how do we harness it to our advantage? Courage is the act of doing something, even when it frightens you. Being afraid is the flight-or-fight reaction we get when we are trapped in a bad situation. This is a normal automatic response for any human – it has evolved in our species for millions of years, and it has helped keep us alive. Whoever tells you they have never been afraid is lying to you. Although fear is something we all experience, it does not have to stop you from reaching your goals. This is where courage comes in.

Courage is simply moving forward (or even through) something, while you are afraid. Imagine courage as our ever-evolving monkey brain meeting modern human logical thought. We can have a flight-or-fight response to something (that's the monkey), but then decide whether to act (that's the human). A person can be afraid and still move forward using courage for any number of reasons. Soldiers in the armed forces use courage to enter the battlefield and defeat the enemy. This is the version of courage most people think of when they think of courage. A soldier is human and so they are afraid of entering a situation that could take their life. Their courage is what gets them through the fear and has them continue forward with their mission.

      While the potential loss of life is reason enough to use courage, there are other less deadly occasions that can demonstrate someone's courage. Imagine the person whose aim is to become stronger in life or at work. Perhaps they have been afraid to speak up or to state their opinion. Perhaps they have taken enough verbal or physical abuse from others. This person perhaps has a fear of confrontation, or they are afraid they will be fired for speaking up. These facts have made them passive, mindlessly agreeing with everyone to avoid arguments. As a Warrior, this person can draw upon the courage in their heart to face a confrontation and make their voice heard.

      We could also consider the person forced into a frightening situation because of their circumstances, and they have no choice but to be courageous. Consider the person who needs a heart transplant to survive. Do they automatically become courageous, just because they need to have an operation? In many ways this person has been forced into being courageous. While I and much of society may call this person brave, courage comes from within, and it can be used to confront this type of situation using a Warrior Mindset.

In 2018 I had brain surgery to alleviate the symptoms of Parkinson's disease. This surgery involved placing two thin, metal rods straight through my brain to the very base of the brain. Many people called me courageous, believing I was brave to just consider this type of operation. Although the surgery is now performed widely and is mostly safe, there is always a 5% chance of something going wrong. In addition, I was told that I would have cognitive issues after the surgery, since the doctors inserted their rods straight through my brain's memory center. Although I was afraid, I thought to myself, *what choice do I have*? The more frightening option would have been living without the surgery. I had no choice but to be courageous.

When you demonstrate your courage in the face of great difficulty, you are in good company. In fact, you are in the company of great men and women, also thrust into their situation through no fault of their own. One excellent example of courage is when 600 marchers led by John Lewis crossed the Edmund Pettus Bridge in Selma, Alabama in 1965. They were non-violent protestors who wanted to demonstrate for their civil rights. As they were about to cross the bridge, named for a confederate general, they were met by troopers wearing gas masks and holding clubs and night sticks. John Lewis stood his ground using every ounce of courage he could muster, though later he would claim he was not afraid. The troopers began pushing the protestors back, clubbing and tear gassing them as they went. Lewis and the others never retaliated, and he was soon knocked to the ground and beaten. Television cameras had recorded the whole thing, and when the public saw the film, it became a turning point in the Civil Rights Movement.

  Your Journey will not always be frightening. In some cases, you will not have to be courageous until the later parts of your Journey. When someone starts a new company, they know that certain risk is involved, but it may not be until they sign the expensive office lease or the very large contract with a client that courage must be used to calm the nerves and allow for success. Sometimes you will need to overcome your own fear of becoming successful. I have been struck with this very fear in the past. The fear is that you will fail, but that you will succeed, and it will change your life. This is a real fear people do not talk about but should. It may take all your courage to put a second note on your house to stabilize your business, but you do it because you are a Warrior, responsible not only to yourself, but to your customers, employees, the bank, and your family. Remember, there can be no courage if you are not afraid.

    Another story of courage is that of Anne Frank, a girl only 14 years of age, who hid with her family in a home in The Netherlands as her country was being occupied by German Nazis. Much of we learn of Anne Frank is from her diary, which she wrote in hiding. She showed incredible courage by writing about both the terrible things happening around her, as well as about the normal things 14-year-olds think about. In 1944 her family was discovered, and they were all sent to concentration camps. Anne died just months before the end of the war. This is another instance of having demonstrated courage in the face of unescapable horror. She had no choice but to be courageous, and she was until the very end.

It has already been said, but it is worth repeating; courage cannot exist without fear. We are all afraid of something in life: being rejected by a loved one, failing at something, succeeding at something (one can surely be afraid of success!), losing money, or losing life or limb. Sometimes we enter situations of our own choosing – deciding to run for office, for example. But sometimes we are thrust into situations that define us because of our courage – staying strong during an illness, as an example. Charles Lindbergh chose to fly a plane across the Atlantic, but it does not mean he was not afraid of failure. Certainly, he was. Mother Teresa chose to live with the most impoverished people in India, but I am sure she was afraid for her safety and for those she knew. Those first responders on 9/11 had no choice but to show courage, and neither did those on Flight 93, also on 9/11. They disabled several terrorists and saved the US Capitol and potentially hundreds of lives. They were afraid, but they all found the courage within them to do what must be done.

Just like with other Warrior traits, courage can be trained like a muscle, to call upon it when you need it most. There are things you can do daily, from trying food you have never tried before, to engaging in a new activity, to doing something a little scary like skydiving for the first time or helping a person or animal in need. These are daily situations you can put yourself in to strengthen your courage muscles. They require no action by anyone else – only you are required to act to set these into motion. What is your first response when someone asks you for change on the street? How do you feel about going to a new restaurant and trying a dish you would normally never order? What would you feel going to a local city council meeting and making public comments about an issue you believe in? Do you make small talk with the barista at the café or the checker at the supermarket? All these situations take courage, and only require you to act, no one else. I am asking you to be open to new experiences, ones that scare you.

  Of course, there are other situations that may arise and which are out of your control. These situations help to test your courage and recognize any areas that may still need work. For example, asking for a promotion at work, standing up for yourself when you feel you have been wronged, leaving an abusive relationship (romantic or otherwise), or standing up for someone else who is being bullied. These are situations that we are forced into, situations that are thrust upon us without our asking for them. These situations allow us to act out of instinct and help demonstrate how much we have developed our courage muscles, or how much more refinement they may need. These situations force us to act and react in the moment. You either jump in and act on something, or you do not. These are also situations that make us think back and ask ourselves, *Why didn't I react? How would I react differently if I could do it over?* We have all been in these situations – the kind that are so unusual, that we fail to act. Maybe we are caught off guard, or we are surprised this is happening – like someone being called a derogatory name right in front of us. The next time you are caught in this situation, *act*, be courageous! Say what you feel is right, even if you think back and believe you could have acted differently. Use your courage to be the change you want in the world!

In short, Warriors are courageous. We are all afraid of something but overcoming what we fear may be the only path forward. It may be difficult to jump off a cliff into the water 20 feet below but doing it will bring you a sense of accomplishment like no other. Whether you stand at the cliff and can decide when to jump, or someone pushes you in, take the leap, overcome fear, and you will be growing your Warrior Mindset!

Persistence

When things are going well, we do not typically think of persistence as a necessary attribute. For example, you do not need persistence to achieve your daily activities or to do things you typically do every day. However, persistence becomes important when things are not going well, or you are about to fail or have failed. Persistence is the act of continuing your effort towards a goal despite roadblocks, challenges, and even failure.

It is easy to move forward doing what you have always done. If you are an educator, continuing the path of educator will not allow you to grow or enhance your ability to be persistent. When your goal requires no effort to achieve, your persistence will not be challenged. The Warrior almost always seeks to be more: a better educator, a better person, etc. Warriors make goals for themselves, and they put themselves in situation in which allows them to grow. They do this with the full knowledge that the only way to grow and to break from the status quo is to put their bodies, minds, and souls into something, even if they know that failure is a potential outcome.

The road to achieving your goal is a part of your story, and adventure awaits the Warrior who puts themselves in a position to grow. I know many authors who love the idea of being published, and I also know a lot of politicians that love the idea of being elected to office. I also know of many businesspeople who dream of the day that they will hit on something big and be rewarded. But many of these people look forward to the reward with little regard to the Journey involved in reaching that goal. They think of the result in which they are published, in Congress, or running a successful business, respectively. These people do not regard the day-to-day highs and lows as important as the result.

The truth is that there will be ups and downs in any endeavor and being involved and knowing how to overcome the detailed challenges will serve you well in the long run. Let us be clear: you will encounter failure, however big or small it is, as a part of your larger plan but continuing to climb that hill is important for several reasons. First, the more experience you have and failure you encounter, the stronger and more knowledgeable you will become as time goes on. An expert sommelier did not become an expert with wines by passing an online course and framing their certificate. They did so by smelling and sampling thousands of wines, understanding the production process, and by hearing feedback from customers and other wine connoisseurs. Each wine they poured, each piece of feedback they heard, grew their power of persistence, and made them less likely to fail in the future.

It is certainly a fact that many people try something but give up when things become difficult. They invest in a camera, take beautiful pictures, but give up when the first photo gallery turns them down. The world is filled with stories of *could have been*, which ended when things became too difficult. I am guilty of such situations in which persistence was needed to reach the next plateau. I once wanted to be a filmmaker, making fictional films and winning awards. Unfortunately, I decided it was too difficult to break through into the top tier, with too much competition that was many times more talented than I was. I gave up on that dream because I was afraid – I lacked courage, the courage to be great, and the persistence needed to achieve my dream.

Fortunately, it is never too late to create a riveting film, and I have been working to create short films to enter small festivals – a far cry of my dream at age 25, but a respectable ambition at this time, with its own challenges to overcome.

    An example of persistence I enjoy using is that of Ray Croc, who turned McDonald's from a single location burger shack into a multi-billion dollar internationally known brand, and whose Journey of persistence was fictionalized in the film *The Founder*. At age 55, Ray was an over-the-hill milkshake machine salesperson. He had tried many business endeavors throughout his adult life but was met with failure. One day, he happened to be selling milkshake makers and encountered a small family-owned restaurant called McDonalds. The restaurant had long lines of people waiting to buy simple and inexpensive hamburgers. It was an efficient operation that sold burgers, fries, and sodas in a novel way. Croc noticed the opportunity, and got on board with the McDonald brothers, eventually buying them out and using a novel franchise model to open new locations. His promise to customers was consistency – any time you entered a

McDonalds, you would have the same experience with the service, the food, and the price.

Ray Croc's persistence paid off, which proved several things. First, the longer you are in the fight and persisting to find an opportunity, the more the odds are in your favor that you will encounter an opportunity that will suit you. Second, it does not matter your age, your ability, your background, or any other was we use to categorize people, if you are persistent at the right goal, you will eventually reach some level of success. Third, do not let your failures define you. As billionaire Mark Cuban once said, *all you need to do is be right once*, meaning you can have a thousand failures preceding your one great success.

Another example of persistence I enjoy is the story of the book, *Chicken Soup for the Soul*, a self-help book written as multiple short stories. The author, Jack Canfield, famously claims to have presented the book to 144 publishers and received 144 rejections. No literary agent would take on the project, afraid it would not sell, and they would lose valuable time and money promoting a type of book not popular at the time. Canfield has told his story of persistence for many years. He took his rejected book to a publisher's fair in California. There were nearly 4,000 publishers at the fair, and he and his co-authors presented the book to what seemed like each company. They kept receiving rejections, but this time in person, which certainly hurts more and made them feel like giving up. Finally, a small publisher said they were interested in publishing the book.

The publisher then asked Canfield how many books he expected to sell – the publisher suggested 20,000 copies – to which Canfield replied he wanted to sell a million and a half copies in one and a half years. His publisher literally laughed in his face. Canfield had a plan and would use his persistence to meet his goal. The book has gone on to sell millions of copies, has been translated into dozens of languages, and has spawned a series of books with similar stories under the Chicken Soup brand. The message here is clear. When others shut their doors to you, you must continue searching for new doors to open. Never take *no* for an answer. That *no* may be more about what someone else is thinking and feeling than what you or your cause is worth. As the saying goes, *one person's trash is another's treasure*. If you believe in your cause, your goal, your challenge to overcome, eventually you will get through the failures and find success.

Just as with all of the qualities of a Warrior, persistence takes practice. In fact, whenever you practice persistence, you are being persistent! There are many ways in which you can stretch and grow your persistence muscles, all of which can be situations you can put yourself into simply for the thrill of practicing your skills.

The first way to practice persistence is by repeating your efforts for the same cause: quite literally the definition of persistence. However, we will discuss it here as practicing on small, low-value propositions. I know of one person who is fighting dementia by completing the newspaper crossword every single day. She has battled through many of the heartbreaking symptoms of dementia by completing daily tasks that help shape her schedule and help her be accountable to herself. Crosswords in the morning, which will lead into lunchtime, followed by a language lesson on her smartphone, followed by exercise, and finally topped off by playing a casual game on her smartphone. She is sure to do this every day without fail, even on the bad days when she will take double the time to complete her crossword puzzle, which pushes every other activity back. She attributes this persistent behavior to her slow progression.

      A persistent person learns from their mistakes and discovers new and better ways to tackle the same problem by changing their strategies and tactics. Just like a gamer might take a different approach to pass a level she had previously failed, anyone who practices flexibility and creativity in subsequent attempts will garner different results. I have a friend who is an investor in start-up companies. He told me that he expects most of these companies will fail in the first year. He understands this, and with each failure he learns more lessons for investing in future companies. Once he invested tens of thousands of dollars on a start-up he believed in, but which had only one founder. When the company failed, his instinct told him that if the company had had two or more founders, it would have had a higher chance of succeeding. The next time he made an investment, he immediately declined solo founders, or paired two very promising founders together on a single project. This change in strategy saw his success rate and return on investment increase by over 50%. Each subsequent attempt is a learning opportunity, and persistent people learn from their mistakes and move forward instead of giving up.

Another way to practice persistence is to model someone successful or rely on the advice of someone successful. Find someone you admire in any area for which you desire a Warrior Mindset, read their biography, and reach out to them online. Ask them questions, follow them on social media, figure out what made them a success in their area of expertise. If you are a student, you may try asking your tutors what persistence skills they used to succeed at school. If you are ill, you may ask someone with the same illness what keeps them going every day. If you are starting a business, find a mentor who has been in business for 20 or 30 years, and ask them how they have kept going for so long. Everyone is different, and you will find your own success by your own means, but the idea of a mentor is still a useful one. Along the way, you will learn lessons of persistence, of failing repeatedly but eventually succeeding, because they never gave up. Their success, after all, is why you seek their advice!

One more way I offer for you to improve your persistence is to take a page out of the book of the Stoics.

Stoicism is an ancient Greek school of thought created by Zeno of Citium. Stoicism teaches the development of self-control and internal strength as a means of overcoming destructive emotions. You can read more about stoicism online (much has been written on the topic) but suffice to say that it is a way to control your emotions so they do not lead to extremes. When you have a success, celebrate with humility, knowing that a failure may be just around the corner. Likewise, when you encounter failure, seek to approach it with humility and with an open mind to understand your mistakes. Stoicism is meant to avoid emotional extremes, like anger and depression and extreme joy and elation. This is to not to say you should not celebrate the wins and be disappointed with the losses but do both in moderation. Life is full of ups and downs, and when you are persistent, you will encounter both.

      Persistence is important for any Warrior. Keep going. Keep moving forward. Learn from your mistakes. Try, and try again. These are the tenets of persistence, an important skill for any Warrior who wants to go far in their pursuits. Attitude is everything; never give up.

Resilience

Resilience is often confused with persistence, and although they are related, they are very different. While persistence entails not giving up after failure, resilience concerns the attitude one takes after defeat. Bouncing back is not just about persisting, but also about returning to a hurdle or challenge with new ideas and an all-in attitude, ready to use the lessons learned to continue moving forward with your pursuit. Resilience is about adapting to a new situation and approaching it with strength. Even though life can lead us into unplanned, and often unfair, situations we often have no choice but to bounce back.

In fact, resilience is so important in our lives, that it is a built-in function of our humanity. Our ancestors who lived in the wild hunted, gathered, were attacked by predators, and had terrible deaths. Because the past's wild nature was filled with so much uncertainty – a group hunt for food could have easily lead to several injuries or deaths – resilience became a defense mechanism to keep our species moving forward and propagating. As such, those who were most resilient, mated with resilient partners, and lead to resilience being engraved into our

DNA. Although we are no longer prey in the wild, we still have the capacity to experience loss and sadness, but with that comes the capacity to continue moving forward.

I have several friends who have unfortunately lost their partner to illness. Sometimes the illness was sudden, and the loss happened quickly, and sometimes the illness took years to progress. In either case, the partner that was left alive took time to grieve their loss (everyone grieves differently and for different lengths of time) and managed to bounce back from their loss. While unfortunate, the partner had no choice but to move forward, for themselves and for their families. Nobody can fully understand the agony and pain of losing a partner unless they have been through it but overcoming the daily struggle of ongoing grief is possible with resilience. And just as with the fact that everyone grieves in different ways, the resilient bounce back will be different for each person. However, be assured that the capacity to bounce back is possible, through personal growth and with courage.

Many of the strategies involved in improving resilience involve other qualities of the Warrior Mindset. One such strategy is to embrace thoughts of courage, strength, and adaptability. We all experience negative thoughts from time to time. It is important to recognize when a thought is negative and not let it get away from you. Many who fall into serious depression allow negative thoughts to take over their minds and this starts a downward spiral. Keep your thoughts in perspective related to the bigger picture. The failure of a business or the failing of a class are not the end of the world. Often, the consequences are not as terrible as they seem. One must have the strength to accept failure and accept the change that it brings. By learning from our past, we can look forward with new ideas and tools that will help us succeed at the next hurdle.

      Another strategy to improve your resilience is to foster wellness. Your body, mind, and soul are all affected when you are reeling from a loss and experiencing stress. This could take a further toll on your overall well-being. For some, fostering wellness may come in the form of exercising more, eating well, spending time with those who are compassionate and empathetic to your cause, and by practicing mindfulness. Mindfulness is an important skill to develop. Sitting silently with your thoughts, praying or meditating, practicing yoga or tai-chi, and opening your mind by taking in the moment with each of your senses, can all improve your mood and prepare you to overcome your challenge. The most important thing here is to avoid negative thoughts and negative actions that lead to negative outcomes. Be aware of your behavior and note any changes you may feel from day to day. If you notice yourself falling into behaviors like substance abuse, risky endeavors (gambling, etc.), or isolation, speak with a therapist to seek help. Seeking help with mental health issues is not a weakness, but an incredibly positive act of courage and resilience.

      Before you are ready to overcome your challenge – including moving forward after a failure, loss, or negative outcome – move slowly and catalog your thoughts. How do you feel differently not from when you undertook the challenge? What have you learned because of this attempt? Be objective: is your advice to yourself sound? Someone who went into business with a partner may want to avoid partnerships in the future. They have *gotten burned* in the past. Is this a sound argument? A more appropriate analysis may be that this business partner was not a good fit for your business. Perhaps instead of dismissing business partners as a rule, dig deeper to discover why this partnership failed. The same goes with romantic partners. If your marriage unfortunately failed, saying *marriage was not for me* is not a sound approach to the problem. Try instead to pinpoint the reason this marriage ended. Be specific in your analysis. If you are a student who is *bad at math*, you may find it simpler to say *I'm just bad at math* than to find out the true reason behind your failure, which may come down to having a bad teacher or utilizing bad study habits.

    I love telling the story of the *latent math genius* when discussing resilience. There was once a student who thought she was *not good at math*. She barely passed her high school mathematics courses and avoided college because every degree program required a basic level of Algebra. To this student, this was the death knell. After taking some classes that she enjoyed, she dropped out of college, realizing that even to become a fashion designer, which was her dream career, she needed to pass that Algebra requirement. She was smart, but never at math. Many years passed, and she was unhappy in her career in retail. She told herself that she needed a change. Her partner also worked in retail, and if they were to get married and have children one day, they would need to earn a larger income to support their lifestyle. She decided that to get to where she wanted to be with her career, she needed a college diploma. She decided to sign up for an arithmetic course at a local community college. She remembered arithmetic and thought this course would be a good refresher for her. She realized that the work was not so difficult as she had imagined. She told her story to the teacher, a full-time math professor. The professor told her, *I'm going to tell you exactly how to pass this class, and every math class in the future.*

    The student was on pins and needles and said she would do anything to succeed at math. The math teacher first asked the student if her high school math teachers also taught a different subject at the school. She said that yes, one teacher also taught yearbook and photo, and another was the basketball coach. The math professor said *only learn math from teachers who love math and only teach math*. Next, the teacher told the student, *there is a math lab every week for students having a tough time in class. Come to it, even if you don't have any questions.* Next, she told the student, *learn to love math – read books about it, watch Good Will Hunting and A Beautiful Mind,* two movies in which the main characters are gifted at math. *You will learn to appreciate math as a subject.* Along with a few other tidbits, the student took the professor's advice. She did well in the beginning of class, but halfway through the course the assignments suddenly became difficult. She had already set herself up to succeed – she was reading books, watching movies, and attending lab every week – so instead of becoming afraid to fail, she looked at the situation as a puzzle to be solved. She started asking questions at math lab and was getting the help she needed from the tutors, many of whom had become her friends. In the end, she passed arithmetic with an *A* grade, and over the next two years she reached Calculus (passing the original math requirement by several levels), and even tutored math at the lab in her spare time while she pursued a computer science degree. Today she works at one of the larger software companies and wears shirts with esoteric math equations to work.

    I recognize that this story was a little longer than the usual stories, but it was worth reading for many reasons. Not only does it demonstrate resilience but also every other aspect of the Warrior Mindset. When you finish this book, return to this story and stop to consider how and why this Warrior came back into control of her life. What qualities does she exhibit that make her a Warrior?

Determination

Determination is defined as having a firm or fixed intention on a goal. It involves keeping yourself motivated toward your goal, and not stopping until reaching it. It differs from resilience and perseverance in that with determination, you have made a choice to be firm on your decision, and that you believe that nothing can stop you. In short, determination is a force inside yourself that keeps you moving toward a goal. Without determination, the initial decision to live, to graduate, to succeed, to win, to be proud, is not made. At times, we find ourselves in situations not of our own making, and we are able to persevere because our attitude does not let us give up. However, with determination, you are resolute, you are actively telling yourself and the universe that you are unstoppable.

Many find determination a short-lived ability that ebbs and flows depending on the situation. Most goals or challenges are difficult, especially if they are worth spending your time on, and so the initial motivation and energy you put forth wanes over time. An example is losing weight or getting fit. Often, we begin by telling ourselves that we are determined to succeed. "This time will be different," or "I need to do this for my long-term health." Who cannot say that long term health is not motivation enough? However, even with best intentions, after a week or two we begin to ease up on our determination and begin falling back to old habits. The motivation to succeed has gone away and you are left with disappointment.

The proper way to use determination is by planning for short-term milestones that are achievable. In the example of getting fit, start by deciding on a small, easily achievable goal for a week. *I will work out every other day for 10 minutes* or *I will eat fewer sugary snacks for a week.* After you have decided to overcome this small challenge, you can track your progress and stay on track. By the time the motivation and determination have gone, you have finished your short-term goal and laid a foundation for further small goals. To maintain your determination, go back to your *raison d'être* and to the *why* you began with on your Journey.

Determination is often seen as synonymous with *will power*, and with good reason. When we think about will power, we often think about the ability to push through a situation, no matter how difficult, using brute force if necessary. There are obvious faults with using brute force to get through something difficult – the inevitable pain and suffering, as well as the potential missteps and losses that accompany a brute force plan of action. Often there is no plan at all, simply to push through and *make it happen*. There are also obvious benefits to using will power and having a *I will push through this* attitude. Often, the strength we draw upon for will power is not available to us in any other form.

    The classic example of will power is the story of someone not capable of lifting more than 100 pounds, for lack of strength, or for whatever other reason. But this same person, faced with a life-or-death situation, perhaps saving a loved one from beneath a small car, will draw will power from deep inside and will allow them to lift a 1,500-pound car off of the person. We often hear of these superhuman feats, and they often draw on will power and sheer determination. As mentioned already, determination is better used in small amounts to reach short goals or milestones. It is doubtful that someone who can lift a car off a loved one can do so 20 times in a row.

Therefore, using will power is useful in small spurts, and works best on smaller challenges and hurdles as milestones.

Of course, when many of us are confronted with a situation in which we are personally threatened, it is easy to panic and approach the challenge instinctively rather than with a calm attitude. In these situations – *If you don't lose weight your life will be shortened, if you don't study for this test, you will fail and subsequently fail the class* – it is easy to use determination to use brute force to overcome this challenge. The patient who is pre-diabetic may attempt to solve the problem by going on a crash diet and do nothing but exercise. Or the college student may attempt to cram for the test, learning an entire term's worth of material in one night. These approaches are unproductive and often lead to failure.

The more prudent approach is to use determination and will power to develop short term goals or tasks to reach the ultimate objective. As the saying goes, *Rome was not built in a day*. This method will help you avoid feeling overwhelmed when approaching your challenge or situation. We can re-write these stories using a more methodical, deterministic approach. With our patient who is pre-diabetic and must lose weight to avoid a shorter life, a more prudent approach would be to set a broad goal, then set milestones for attaining that broader goal. For example, they may start by cutting sugars from their diet for a week. The next week, they can add 15 minutes of exercise. The third week they can cut out fried foods. The fourth week they can increase their exercise to 30 minutes. Incremental, prescribed steps will help keep the patient determined to succeed.

With our student, let us assume they really have gone all term without studying and must now cram that knowledge in one night. Obviously, this is a bad place from which to begin, and the student should have anticipated the level of work involved. But with only hours until the final, they are best served by developing a realistic objective – pass the class – which may entail simply earning a 2.0 grade point average (or a C) in the class. They can plan to dedicate an hour per chapter the night before the exam, familiarizing themselves with the essential concepts of each unit or chapter. Finally, before the test, they may do an overall review of the material. Breaking the goal into smaller tasks is the surefire way to avoid becoming overwhelmed along the way.

Just as with the other Warrior skills, determination can be improved upon. First, approach any challenge or goal from a place of strength by focusing on your own strengths, and minimizing your exposure to your weaknesses. If you have difficulty with learning from a textbook, you may be a visual learner, and learning from online video courses may be a better fit for you. If you do better when surrounded by other people, then engage in activities that will help you reach your goal while being around people. I once knew of a novelist who could only write her books while sitting at a café around people. The only way she could concentrate was being in a noisy environment with a lot of people moving in and out all day.

Always depend on your deliberate choices and actions rather than relying on luck. During the vaccination phase of the pandemic, the people who received their vaccines first in each group were the ones who were proactive, checking message boards for clues on where to receive the vaccine rather than depending on luck of being called by their healthcare provider. Luck and hope are not useful strategies. Proper planning and proactive determination are the paths forward.

You will find that other Warrior abilities and values intersect with determination. For example, bringing focus to a task will help avoid distractions. Perseverance is helpful if your determination is flailing, offering encouragement so that you may continue forward.

Adaptive

Adaptability is an important skill to master if you are to become a Warrior. Being adaptive means being able to adjust to changing circumstances or conditions. In nature we see that the most successful species of animals are the ones that adapt best to their situation. One example of adaptation in human history is the way our early ancestors adapted to changing environments as they migrated out of Africa.

Around 2.5 million years ago, our early human ancestors, homo habilis, lived in Africa and were primarily scavengers and had a diet of fruits, nuts and insects. However, as the climate changed and the African savannah began to dry out, food became scarce, forcing early humans to adapt. One adaptation was the development of stone tools, which allowed them to access new food sources such as meat from animals they hunted.

This marked the beginning of the Stone Age and the shift towards a more diverse diet.

As the climate continued to change, early humans began to migrate out of Africa in search of new environments and resources. They made their way into Europe and Asia, where they encountered new challenges such as colder temperatures and different types of animals. To survive in these new environments, early humans had to adapt. One of the most notable adaptations was the evolution of Homo erectus, who had a larger brain, more advanced tools, and the ability to control fire. This allowed them to hunt large animals and survive in colder climates.

Another adaptation was the development of clothing and shelter. Early humans began to make use of animal skins and furs to keep warm and constructed shelters to protect themselves from the elements. They also developed new hunting techniques, such as using traps and working together as a group, to hunt larger and more dangerous animals.

As time passed, early humans continued to adapt and evolve. They developed new technologies such as the bow and arrow, which allowed them to hunt more efficiently, and began to domesticate plants and animals. This led to the development of agriculture and the rise of permanent settlements.

The human ability to adapt and evolve has been crucial to our survival as a species. From the earliest days of our ancestors to the present, we have had to adapt to changing environments and circumstances to survive. Through ingenuity, creativity and cooperation, humans have been able to overcome the challenges they have faced and continue to thrive.

Today we do not have to worry about the dangers our ancestors faced. We discovered energy beyond simple fire, which allowed us to have heating and air conditioning, and which cooks our food and runs our vehicles. We live in the most technologically advanced period of human history, and so we have lost a lot of what made us human in the first place. Today, we do not need to adapt like in caveman days. The most significant form of adapting we do these days does not lead to life-or-death situations. For many, adapting simply means choosing to have a hot tea or a warm soup on an upset stomach. So, in many ways we have lost the ability to adapt to the natural world around us.

Another example of adaptation in history is the way the ancient Maya civilization adapted to their environment. The Maya lived in an area that was prone to drought, and they had to find ways to survive in a harsh environment with limited resources.

One way the Maya adapted was through their agricultural practices. They developed an advanced system of terrace farming, which allowed them to make the most of the limited fertile land available. They built terraces on the steep hillsides, which prevented soil erosion and maximized the amount of land that could be used for farming. They also developed a complex system of irrigation, using canals and dams to control the flow of water to their crops. These innovations allowed the Maya to grow a wide variety of crops, including corn, beans, and squash, which were the staples of their diet.

Another way the Maya adapted was through their architecture. They built their cities and pyramids with the local limestone and volcanic rock, which were abundant in the area. They also used a technique called corbelling to construct the walls of their buildings, which allowed them to build taller structures without the use of mortar. This technique allowed them to create impressive architectural feats such as the pyramids of Tikal and Uxmal.

The Maya also adapted to their environment through their religious beliefs. They believed that the gods controlled the forces of nature, and they developed a complex system of rituals and ceremonies to appease the gods and bring rain during times of drought. They also built elaborate ceremonial centers, such as the Temple of the Sun at Palenque, where they performed these rituals.

As we can see, adapting to new situations has always been the norm for humans from all societies. Let us look at a more modern example of adaptation with the story of Mahatma Gandhi.

Gandhi was a political and spiritual leader in India during the early 20th century, who fought for India's independence from British colonial rule. At the start of his political career, Gandhi employed peaceful civil disobedience tactics, such as boycotts and non-violent protests. However, as the independence movement gained momentum and the British government grew more resistant, Gandhi realized that he needed to adapt his approach.

To succeed, Gandhi turned to more extreme forms of non-violent resistance such as fasting and campaigns of mass civil disobedience. He also worked to unite India's diverse population and religious communities under the common goal of independence. Through his tireless efforts and ability to adapt his strategies, Gandhi played a key role in India's eventual independence in 1947. His legacy lives on as a champion of non-violent resistance and a symbol of peaceful social change.

One last example is that od Alexander the Great. He was a king of Macedon, a state in ancient Greece, and one of the greatest military leaders in history. At the start of his career, Alexander was a skilled warrior and tactician who led his army to victory in many battles. However, as he expanded his empire and conquered new territories, he faced new challenges and different cultures.

To succeed, Alexander had to adapt his leadership style and military strategies. He learned the languages and customs of the peoples he conquered and appointed local leaders to govern in his name. He also adopted the customs and practices of the conquered people, to gain their loyalty and respect. Through his ability to adapt and his military genius, Alexander was able to create one of the largest empires in history, stretching from Greece to India. He is remembered for his military tactics, his administrative and political acumen, and his cultural achievements.

Now that we have read about some examples of adaptability from history, let us look at the strategies you can use to be more adaptive.

Embrace a growth mindset. A growth mindset is the belief that you can develop your abilities and achieve your goals through effort and learning. This mindset allows you to view challenges and setbacks as opportunities for growth and development, rather than as insurmountable obstacles. To develop a growth mindset, focus on learning from your experiences, experimenting with new approaches, and seeking out feedback and mentorship.

Develop a diverse skill set. Having a wide range of skills and knowledge makes you more adaptable because it allows you to approach problems from different perspectives and find new solutions. To develop a diverse skill set, take on different types of projects, seek out new learning opportunities, and broaden your experience by working in different industries or roles.

Be open to change. Being adaptable requires being open to change and willing to try new things. This means being willing to let go of old ways of thinking and doing things and being willing to take risks and try new approaches. To become more open to change, practice being open-minded and curious, and actively seek out new experiences and perspectives.

Build a strong network. Having a strong network of contacts and connections can help you to be more adaptable because it gives you access to a wide range of perspectives, skills, and resources. To build a strong network, focus on building relationships based on trust, mutual support, and shared goals. Make a point of connecting with people from different backgrounds and industries and stay in touch with your network on a regular basis.

Learn to be flexible. Flexibility is key to being adaptable. It means being able to adjust your plans and approach as circumstances change and being able to work effectively under pressure. To develop flexibility, focus on developing your problem-solving and decision-making skills, and practice being comfortable with uncertainty and ambiguity.

Develop emotional intelligence. This means being able to recognize, understand, and manage one's own emotions and the emotions of others. Emotional intelligence allows individuals to be more adaptable as they are better able to navigate difficult situations, communicate effectively, and build relationships. To develop emotional intelligence, individuals should focus on developing their self-awareness, empathy, and social skills.

In short, being adaptable is a key trait for success in today's rapidly changing world. By implementing these strategies, you can become more equipped to handle new challenges and opportunities as they arise, and ultimately, be more successful in awakening your Inner Warrior.

Focused

One Warrior attribute that is often minimized, though not completely overlooked, is the importance of being focused on one's pursuits. Just as you cannot see direct evidence of a black hole unless you observe the cosmic debris around it, you often cannot see the result of being focused, but you can certainly observe the result of an unfocused mind. To bring focus into your life, you must know yourself enough to know what distracts you from your main goal. Often, these distractions are just ways of procrastinating, keeping yourself from doing what is important instead of what is convenient.

A Warrior understands that distraction is the killer of productivity, and an unfocused mind cannot attain success in any single pursuit. Therefore a Warrior Mindset must include focus. The Warrior must drop all distractions from their lives and focus on the main goal or objective. You may have heard the phrase *jack of all trades but master of none*. This refers to the person who puts their attention and inclinations onto too many activities. With such limited time in life, one cannot master anything without dedication and repetition, which requires focus. Some say it takes 10,000 or 50,000 hours to master an activity. But how many usable hours are in a day? Let us assume we are awake for 16 hours (reserving 8 hours for sleep), and we are focused on our goal or success on our given path. This would require a minimum of 625 days and a maximum of 3,125 days to master an activity.

It can be argued that focus on a continual basis, every day, for that many days is impossible. It Is not impossible, simply look at the monks of medieval times who dedicated their entire lives to praying. One can argue that these monks used an intense focus to do nothing with their lives but pray, which they believed was of the utmost importance. They did so from the moment they woke up until the moment they went to sleep. Of course, if your goal is to be a monk, then this would be a very different book. This book considers the various needs of daily life that pull us in different directions. None of us can remain focused on one activity for too long, no matter how much it means to us or how important it is in our lives. Therefore, focus is so important, especially when attempting to develop a Warrior Mindset. For us, focus is an action that happens over time rather than daily for x-number of hours.

What you choose to focus on is as important as what not to focus on. Think about how you spend your day. Make a daily schedule for yourself using pencil and paper. You wake up, you prepare breakfast, you shower, you go to school or work, you come home, you eat again, etc. Everyone will have a different schedule. Some may be in physical therapy all day, while other may be at school running from class to class, while others will roll out of bed to their computers and spend the day there. Everyone is different, but what everyone has in common is that there are some things that can be unfocused to bring other things into focus. If your goal is to finish college with high marks, you may want to rethink joining the various clubs and or a fraternity if doing so makes your grades suffer. If you are running a startup while also working a second job to earn some income, it may be worth considering what impact one hour less at your regular job may have on your startup, giving it one more hour of your time per day.

Some call the concept of focus *minimalism*. What impact would lowering your workload have on your overall life. In this situation, we don't want to minimize, but rather prioritize. To use an example from business, in 1995, then Apple Computer was reeling from the losses. A decade earlier the board had voted out founder Steve Jobs, and the company had leadership that did not understand what customers wanted. The company released model after model of Mac computer, many with similar specifications that were difficult to compare. During this time, the company had also begun licensing its software to third party hardware manufacturers, so the market was full of these Mac clones, which made selecting the appropriate model even more difficult. Customers were confused, which lead to lower sales, and the eventual return of Steve Jobs as CEO. When Jobs came in, he stopped the software licensing deals and focused the dozen or so models of computers down to four models. When he introduced the iPod, he introduced one single model. When he introduced the iPhone, he introduced one model. The same happened to the computer line. One pro model laptop, one consumer laptop, one professional desktop, and one consumer desktop – all configurable, but each fitting a specific customer. With fewer choices and fewer decisions to be made, sales went up. Focus was the key.

      I will share with you another example of focus, which will illustrate the point. I knew of a young man who wanted to earn his master's in business administration (MBA) to advance his career as an accountant. The program was a two-year, full-time program, which meant he would leave his job and focus solely on school. This went well, until he joined a scholastic competition to develop a start-up, which took away from his studies. When his team won the competition, along with $10,000 to put his start-up idea into action, his time was further divided. This took away more time from his studies. He knew he wanted to be involved and help shape the student experience, so he ran for class representative. He was very popular, and he won the seat to represent his class, while his studies languished even more. His honor roll grades of *A* in every class went down to *Bs* and eventually *Cs*. He was overwhelmed by his extracurricular duties along with his classwork, and after the second semester, he dropped out of school, a victim of burnout. Now he had no job, no school, and was in a bad mental and emotional headspace because of his failure. However, this was not the end of the story. After taking a semester off, using savings to travel and clear his mind of all his previous mistakes, he returned to school. Newly focused on schoolwork, he participated in student clubs, but was not involved in running them. His focus on schoolwork put him back on the honor roll, and he graduated with honors a year and a half later. He not only showed an attitude of determination, but of focus as well. By dropping the optional and unnecessary parts of his studies, he was able to focus on what was important, passing his coursework. Today he is a senior accountant at one of the big accounting firms.

For both Apple Computer, as well as the MBA student, focus was the key to their success. They discovered that more did not equal better. Putting their efforts squarely on one main task or line of action would lead to better results in the long run. The alternative was spreading themselves too thin and not making progress on the most desired activity. The idea of focus has been around since civilization itself. Imagine the focus it took to build the great pyramids of Egypt – the Pharaohs had their focus set on one single accomplishment, at great cost of money, labor, and resources. Military commanders have understood focus' power for millennia. Imagine developing a goal for each battle, and each battle with a singular focus to win. *Winning* was assessed and detailed for each battle. This led to strategies and tactics that would lead to a win. If you have ever played a strategy game such as RISK, you understand the importance of focus. If you try to take over the board too soon, you risk spreading yourself too thin and losing land by opposing forces. Instead, if you develop beach heads on a single continent at a time, you can slowly but surely spread yourself out to further territories little by little. Again, focus is the key.

Another great example of focus comes from Olympian, and the most decorated American gymnast of all time, Simone Biles. With 30 gold medals in competition, she is a shining light for the idea of focus in life to reach a goal. To win those medals, she trained incessantly. Her daily routine consisted of waking up at around 7:45am, having breakfast, going to the gym from 9am until noon, returning home for lunch, then heading back to the gym at 3pm until 6pm, then spending time doing therapy to help heal her body. If you think this is a difficult routine, consider the fact that she underwent this routine daily. Her single solitary focus was to win championships, and the strategy of her workout and dietary routine help her develop tactics – the small steps – to reach her goal.

The key to understanding focus is to leave out everything that is non-essential so that only the essential remains. Not everyone has sponsors that allow you to train seven days a week. Not everyone has the time or money to go back to school full time. We must examine our own lives and recognize what is superfluous and what is essential. To me, my partner is essential, especially since she is also my *reason to be*. The people who are closest to you are essential, and while much is made of having solid friendships as well as acquaintances on the periphery of your life, they will understand when you tell them you must say *no* to a particular activity that takes away your time and energy. You must take into consideration all your activities and find out which are essential, and which are not. Apart from the closest people in your life, nothing is sacred when choosing what is non-essential. Watching television and otherwise spending time and money frivolously are non-essential. Eating well and finding time to exercise are essential, since they keep you healthy and keep you going for longer.

Ultimately, you will need to decide what is essential and non-essential so that you may focus on the essential activities to achieve your objective. The following are some strategies you may use to improve your focus on both a large and small scale. We have already discussed the importance of eliminating distractions. A night drinking with friends, binge-watching television shows, and other distractions may feel good at the time, but ultimately, they take away time and resources that are necessary to achieve your broader goals.

A great strategy is to set small, attainable goals to complete each day and which bring you closer to your goal. If you do something each day towards your goal, you are practicing extended focus and using a forward-looking Mindset, which brings you closer to your goal and encourages you to continue moving forward with your goal.

When most people think of focus, they think of the idea of concentration. These two are not the same and should not be confused. Concentration is the intense focus we have on a moment-to-moment basis, and which may be involved when writing a vision document. Let us consider this situation and consider the distractions that multitasking with your computer allows. With multitasking, there is a cost of energy, time, and resources with *switching*. You are writing your vision document, and suddenly an e-mail arrives. You switch to your e-mail, realizing it is just spam. Now you switch back to your vision document and you have lost of your train of thought. This is a simple example of how switching tasks steals you of precious time. This is also an example of concentration versus focus. Concentration is in the moment, but focus is about the bigger picture of how you spend your time each day.

Being focused on your goals and objectives while deprioritizing distractions and things that keep you from your goals, are hugely important for developing a Warrior Mindset. When too many distractions are present, you lose focus on the process. It is important to recognize what is essential, and to leave out distractions that take our most important resource: time. Time is finite, and we must use it wisely.

Awareness

Awareness is often confused with attention but let us explore the difference. When you are aware of yourself and your surroundings, you are examining reality for what it is, or at least with as few blinders on as possible. Attention is simply a type of awareness that is held for a moment or two. In an office meeting, the speaker may have your attention; you are listening to what they say, you are using their speech as input to your brain. However, you are a passive recipient of information in this situation. If we turn the tables and now you are the speaker, you cannot simply say what is on your slide and expect your audience to keep their attention. You must be actively aware and taking input from the audience: a head that nods off, someone playing with their pen. You are constantly aware of how your actions and words affect others. This is an active experience and is the reason public speaking can be so exhausting and mentally draining.

Many people equate awareness with mindfulness and with good reason. Having an awareness of your surroundings, being aware of who you are interacting with and how you are interacting, are all parts of mindfulness. However, the difference between mindfulness and awareness is that with mindfulness, you are *experiencing* life through the senses, while with awareness you are *understanding* life through the senses. While both are active ways to engage with your environment, awareness adds the extra layer of comprehending the situation, and understanding how your actions affect the situation. Some might call this *reading the room* or *self-awareness* or even *emotional intelligence*. In the end, no matter what you call it, you must have an awareness of yourself and how you affect the world if you are to develop a Warrior Mindset.

A Warrior must have awareness of self to understand their own strengths and weaknesses. This is first and foremost when discussing awareness as a part of the Warrior Mindset. A Warrior must know what strengths they bring to the battle. Attributes of one's own history or experience is a strength when it can match the battle at hand. A person may be the world's best conversationalist, but unless they embark on a goal that requires this skill, it is neither a strength nor a weakness. Warriors must also be aware of their weaknesses. Just as with strengths, weaknesses are not truly weaknesses unless they are about the task at hand. If a Warrior finds weakness as someone who cannot endure physical pain, if the challenge ahead does not call for enduring physical pain, then this weakness is irrelevant to the Warrior's Journey.

    A strength can be any skill, knowledge, or experience the Warrior brings to battle, and which is relevant to the Journey. Different skills can be strengths, depending on the battle. For example, a Warrior who is an accountant, and who wants to run their own business, the skill of accounting, as well as the general knowledge of business, are strengths they bring to the table to succeed in their Journey. An ill patient who is taken care of by the best specialists in their area can be considered to bring medical strength to their Journey.

I have a friend who is an actor in Hollywood. I would consider her a Warrior in her Journey to become a well-known actor. Not only are her performances very strong (she was educated by some of the finest acting teachers and coaches in the city), but she also brings the necessary strength of tenacity and grit (must have skills to succeed with longevity in Hollywood). Consequently, since I have known her, going on more than 20 years, she has created incredible performances for professional films and television shows, as well as for student projects. She ceases every opportunity to practice her craft, and as such, she has recently played in some high-profile roles. Her strengths matched the Journey. To succeed in Hollywood, you must be a good actor, have tenacity (which she has in droves), and stay with the Journey throughout the ups and downs.

At the same time, my friend understands her weaknesses in Hollywood, and she understands the reasons she is not yet an Oscar-winning, $20 million-per-film actor. She does have the 'it' factor that many casting directors look for; the smile that can light up a room. However, having been in the industry for as long as she has, she understands the weakness of age and age discrimination in Hollywood that she brings to her career. Her strengths and weaknesses are a part of who she is, and she must be attuned to them both to succeed. She knows she can no longer play a college student, so she seeks roles of the older sister or of a young mother, which has helped her overcome the weakness she faces on her Journey.

Staying with show business, I know another person who used to be a sportscaster on the radio. He has a booming yet smooth voice that captivates his audience. His voice and his love of sports were a part of his Journey into radio and helped him with his career. As it happens, he is also a very good cook and is a very friendly person. These last two qualities, while can be considered strengths in a different context (for example, in dating or other situations), carry no weight as to whether he would succeed as a broadcaster. Last year he was diagnosed with an illness that weakened his voice and took away some of his charisma. His strength (his booming and smooth voice) suddenly became a weakness. Realizing this, he changed jobs, focusing less on using his voice and more on his production skills. He turned his weakness back into a strength since he was hired as producer to work with other on-air personalities.

A Warrior must have awareness of self to understand how they affect the world. When a young girl plays games with her brother in their bedroom, it is safe to say they do not affect the world very much. However, consider an adult with a platform – a politician, a public speaker, a professor, an advocate for a particular illness, a business owner with several employees – these people can all change the world with their words and actions. They have a platform, people are listening to what they have to say, and their words matter. A Warrior must have self-awareness, especially when interacting with the world, since they are likely to change their world.

These days, it may seem that accruing likes on your social media posts means that your voice is being heard. In most cases, this is not true at all, but in other cases it may be truer than we would like to believe. Let us suppose a person with 500 friends or connections on social media makes a post about some policy the government is currently debating. This person posts about how they are for the policy. They may or may not receive likes from friends and followers, but people are seeing the post and perhaps shaping their opinion based on that post. This is how influence happens in real life as well. You may not receive immediate feedback for your opinion, thought, or statement, but others are watching and listening. I cannot tell you how many times I have posted my thoughts on social media, not receive any response about my posting, but later be asked about it in real life. You may have more influence than you think.

For a more concrete example of this, let us consider the words of a reporter on the news. One evening they may make a comment or statement about a news story, and the next day, people may be using those exact words to convey their own beliefs on the same topic. Even though that news reporter cannot see their audience, their audience can see and hear them. The same goes for an owner of a business with several employees. The business owner may or may not think so, but their words carry meaning to their employees, and they can affect morale, job satisfaction, and even an employee's idea about job security. A Warrior must be aware of their words and actions and must not speak or act without consideration for those who may be affected.

As with other Warrior qualities, there are ways to improve awareness, especially self-awareness. The more you practice this skill, the better you will be at using it when the moment arises. This skill can be extremely useful in many situations, so finding a time and place to use this skill is as simple as closing your eyes and feeling your senses in the moment. Here are some more specific ways to practice awareness, especially self-awareness.

Embrace your intuition. Learn about yourself through mindfulness exercises and learn to trust your mind and body. When an unexpected situation comes your way, you will not hesitate to react in the moment, since intuition is something that can use to connect your thoughts with actions in the present moment. If you have experienced moments in your life where you wish you would have reacted differently to a situation, intuition will help you react more timely next time. Trust yourself.

Keep an open mind. Developing self-awareness, using meditation and mindfulness, and getting in touch with yourself may all sound like new age hocus pocus, but believe me, it works. By keeping an open mind, you allow yourself to have a growth mindset that will give you the ability to improve your life and well-being, not to mention become a Warrior. Sometimes the only way to break bad habits and long-held ideologies that have held you back in the past is to stay open to new ways of thinking.

Know your emotional triggers. There are things in our lives that immediately cause us pain, and we must recognize these to overcome them, or at least to not be held captive by them. Sometimes these triggers are as small as a comment a coworker makes about your performance at a meeting, or an instructor's grade on an exam that is less than an *A*, or a comment from a significant other about your clothes fitting oddly lately, or if you are ill and someone comments, *but you don't look sick*. All these triggers can cause us to act irrationally, either outwardly with physical reactions, or inwardly with emotional buildup in our bodies. A Warrior must be aware of these triggers and learn to minimize their effects. Remember, we cannot control the behaviors of others, only our own.

Keep a journal. Journaling is one of the best ways to bring out your own thoughts and emotions. If you do not keep a journal, your own thoughts and ideas will take up psychological space in your mind. Instead, make your thoughts and emotions concrete on paper, thereby liberating your mind from the responsibility of juggling them. Journaling could also help us understand ourselves better, allowing us to share our most intimate thoughts with the paper, which we can later return to for insight into ourselves. You can discover a lot about yourself when you come back to entries you made even just a day or a week ago. This active form of memorializing your thoughts helps bring awareness back to an event or situation that was once ruling your thoughts. This allows you to reflect on your thoughts once more and to consider how best to use that knowledge.

Look at yourself objectively. It can be extremely difficult to look at oneself objectively, but this is a necessary activity for a Warrior. Objectivity comes from objective measures – objective feedback about our performance – so you must remain objective, even if you become emotional. An objective measure can be a test result, or some other objective ruler used to measure an outcome. Other objective measures include a balance sheet, voting results, blood tests, and the bathroom scale. All of these provide you with an objective, un-biased view at your activities. Warriors embrace objectivity because you cannot improve what you cannot objectively measure.

Perform daily self-reflection. Keeping a journal is useful for self-reflection, but it is not the only way one may self-reflect. Before going to bed, you can lay quietly in bed and mentally walk through the major events of the day and consider how those affected you. You may consider analyzing the situation and think about how you might react similarly or differently in the future. The important aspect of this daily self-reflection is to open the pandora's box on your activities, think about them for about five or ten minutes, and then put them back into the box. Do not carry the weight of negative events or situations into the following day. Thinking about these activities daily will help clear your mind for the future and will leave your mind clear for the following day.

Ask for feedback from trusted friends and allies. To truly understand how others see you, you may want to ask for feedback from those who are closest to you. Many times, the people in your life want to appease you and are not likely to say anything too damaging to your ego, but many will agree to be critical of you if you promise you will take the feedback calmly or without becoming angered or holding resentment. If you find someone who knows you and who is willing to hold you up to a mirror and tell you how they really feel about your actions in a particular situation, that person is your champion, and you should listen to their feedback. They are helping you better understand yourself, and there is no person you should rather have at your side.

Disciplined

The actual definition of discipline is training to obey rules or a code of behavior, using punishment to correct disobedience. This is not the way we will define discipline for a Warrior, but this is still an important concept to understand. In our world, a Warrior only answers to themselves through self-discipline. We do not seek outside intervention to keep us on track – that intervention comes from within. The strong desire to fight and achieve success and overcome our obstacles comes from deep inside of us. Only we can have the strength to continue moving forward; nobody can give that strength to us.

Self-discipline can be defined as the ability to stay aligned with one's own self-imposed rules or code of behavior, for risk of losing the Warrior Mindset and failing at the Journey. Self-imposed rules can be as simple as taking a one mile walk every morning or waking up early enough to open your store each day. Self-discipline can be as simple as getting up in the morning, hugging the person closest to you, or as complex as following an intense 8-hour daily fitness routines. These self-imposed rules are critical to our success as Warriors and must be attended to and followed. A code of behavior is not what is taught at finishing school for a lady to be a lady or a gentleman to be a gentleman, but rather moral codes that inform our everyday actions and behaviors. The morals and ethics are set by your intent – intent to succeed at your Warrior activity.

      Students must adhere to the honor code of their schools, disavowing behavior such as cheating, theft, and disruptive activities. Doctors live by the Hippocratic Oath to tend to their patients fairly, and to "first, do no harm." Businesspeople must follow local laws and rules about sanitation, treatment of employees, and taxes. Politicians should live and die by their moral character. Caregivers who stay strong for their loved ones must not show them their pain. There are no shortcuts to success. Self-discipline is behavior that must be repeated often enough to become habit, and that proves dedication to your cause. Can a Warrior exist without the morals and ethics brought about by self-discipline? Yes, but to defy one's code is to defy oneself.

    Defining one's own code is likely the most important act a Warrior can make. The code itself will depend on the Warrior's *raison d'être*, their reason to be, their reason to exist. Many people adapt a Warrior Mindset for what may seem trivial, such as losing weight or becoming fit. This is a perfectly fine reason to attain a Warrior Mindset, but many do not realize that this is a lifelong struggle and is not a goal to be attained and forgotten about in three months. Fitness can be a lifelong struggle for many, as it may involve other behavioral and psychological obstacles to overcome. Others may apply their Warrior skills to specific events or goals, with a limited duration of their activities, such as preparing to run a marathon and then running that marathon.

    In any case, the idea of self-discipline is important no matter what goal you would like to reach or obstacle you would like to overcome. There are several aspects of self-discipline we will discuss here, including the ability to control one's own feelings, the ability to overcome one's own weaknesses, the ability to pursue what one thinks is right despite temptations to abandon it.

The ability to control one's own feelings, and being in touch with those feelings, are key for any Warrior. Knowing what pushes your buttons and makes you angry or upset, and likewise what situations cause you to be happy or excited, is an essential skill worth mastering. This ability to control your own emotions helps you to be more in control of your own body and actions. We have discussed stoicism in other parts of the book – the ability to keep a level temper no matter the situation – but as a part of self-discipline, controlling your feelings in everyday situations will help you connect with people more effectively. Imagine the Warrior who is not outwardly affected when a terminal diagnosis arrives for a loved one, having mastered self-discipline to give their loved one strength. Or imagine the Warrior who can avoid panic in an active shooter situation. These are of course extreme situations – situations we can only hope we are never in. However, we can use these situations as examples that demonstrate the Warrior's ability to stay in control when confronted with a dire situation that they have prepared for.

A Warrior must have the discipline to overcome their own weaknesses when it matters. They must be in control their own mind and body to push through the situation. Imagine yourself running through a gauntlet, with opponents on either side impeding your goal. Most people will see these opponents as their main obstacle. But a Warrior sees the obstacle as a black box – all the Warrior knows is that something is ahead of them, and they must push through it no matter the cost to themselves. This means the Warrior should be prepared to make sacrifices that they are uncomfortable with to reach their goals. If the opponent in the gauntlet is fire, the Warrior must be like water. If the gauntlet presents as an open map with few directions, the Warrior must construct their own map and find a way to make it through.

      Finally, Warriors must find it in them to pursue what is right despite temptations to abandon it. This means the Warrior has a set of morals or ethics, which are based on their *raison d'être*, and these resulting values must be used as the guide for all decisions the Warrior makes, including the discission to abandon or not abandon the Journey. If the values are held to the highest standard, the Warrior will not abandon the Journey, but may instead realign their goals while keeping true to their values.

There are many examples of self-discipline in everyday life, from working diligently to write a book by writing a certain number of words each day, to the story of a young man I'm acquainted with named James, who was trying to get fit. He was 35 years old and had noticed his metabolism slowing over the past several years. James worked at a desk job and finding time to exercise was always an issue. James could find little free time after work, since he prioritized being a good husband and father outside of his job. To give you an idea of his weight, he stood 5 feet 7 inches tall, and weighed 325 pounds. He knew he was not at a healthy weight, but he could not motivate himself even when his doctor confronted him with the possibility of having a stroke. But at 35 years old, James thought a stroke was far off and that he still had time to change his lifestyle. Then one day at work, James' blood pressure jumped through the roof. He had intense pain in his chest and could not move. He was having a heart attack.

As James was being attended to by the ER doctors, he could only think about his family. What if he were to die? Suddenly, the abstract idea of being unhealthy became real and concrete. His doctor told him he could have died, and that if anything, this should serve as a wakeup call. He was put on s variety of medications to control his blood pressure and cholesterol. James needed to change his lifestyle, or he would probably be dead at 40. From that day forward, James committed himself to becoming healthy. His first course of action was to take a 30-minute walk daily. When trying to plan it in his day, he realized he would need to wake up early to exercise. Instead of waking up daily at 7am, he would wake up at 6am and walk for thirty minutes before getting ready for work. This was difficult at first, but it became easier over the coming weeks. He also began eating a low-salt diet – this meant no more fast food, his favorite, and the easiest option for lunch. He began learning about the causes for high cholesterol and eventually became a vegan, talking advantage of the popular *meat made from plants* trend.

    It took incredible discipline to maintain this lifestyle. His wife and daughter saw the change in James' attitude and how fit he was becoming, and decided to join in. Now the entire family was on the *get fit and healthy* train, and soon everyone was feeling much better, with more energy. He also loved that fitness had become a family activity. In a year, James had shed 100 pounds, and was off the medications. He still had a long way to go, but with his *raison d'être* joining in and helping him reach his goals, he was unstoppable. His self-discipline, along with his reason to be made James a Warrior.

Individualistic

At first, it may appear that individualism is not a positive trait, but rather a negative one. We grow up to believe that we are a part of a society, and that we must act in the need of our community. While this may be true, the Warrior Mindset requires us to be individualistic when achieving our individual goals. Someone who is individualistic puts their individual needs before the needs of others. We will see why this is an important value for a Warrior to possesses during their Journey.

Let us begin by considering the opposite of individualism so we can observe why a Warrior must be individualistic. As a Warrior, you are proposing a course of action that will put you at the center of your own Journey. This means that whatever goals a Warrior sets out for themselves must be the top priority, since they are only accountable to themselves. Imagine carrying the weight of your entire community, saying yes to every request by them, rather than focusing on your individual Journey? You would be serving the needs of others rather than your own needs, which must come first if you are to succeed.

University programs in medicine, law, and business are great examples of how individualism can lead to success. Incoming students in those programs are often given a lecture about saying goodbye to friends and family for however many years the programs run. They advise students to *throw a going-away party for yourself* because they will be engulfed in their program until graduation. You must consider your own goals, as well as the costs of interruptions from those around us, if we are to achieve success.

Before we examine the idea of individualism further, let us first define individualism. In our definition, we have more than the self to focus on. Our individualism must be extended to include those around us, especially those who are a part of our *raison d'être*. While it is perfectly fine to be individualistic with your time, efforts, and direction, you must also consider the personal cost of ignoring the time, effort, and direction of those closest to us. Consider these people, perhaps a partner and your children, as a part of your Individual Unit. Your Individual Unit may or may not be a part of your *raison d'être*, however, this Individual Unit must be a part of your Warrior Journey since your life is shared with them.

As an example of the Individual Unit, we can return to the example of intense graduate programs at many universities. While other students in the program as well as deans will suggest incoming students say goodbye to their friends for two (or more) years, this does not include saying goodbye to the Individual Unit. Instead, the most successful programs invite student partners and children to take part in most activities involving their student. My university specifically had programs, which were essentially support groups, for partners. The people in the Individual Unit were able to share in activities that made them feel connected to the larger goal.

Therefore, for this chapter, we will define the Warrior as someone who is a part of the Individual Unit. Here are some examples of how the Individual Unit is important to the Warrior Journey.

In our first example, consider that your goal is to run for public office to be a local councilmember, or to rise even further. There is no doubt that individualism plays a huge role in your decision-making process, in your campaign, and after you are elected. But running for public office is so time consuming and stressful, that to leave behind those in your Individual Unit, you are bound to fall into traps that take time and energy away from those who matter most. Ultimately, you will end up with disgruntled people in that Individual Unit, which could hurt your chances of ever reach your goal of being elected. However, if your *raison d'être* really is political greatness at any cost, then perhaps the lessons in this book are not for you.

    On the other hand, a patient lying in a hospital bed, battling an incurable illness, will have family at the forefront of their mind. Their *raison d'être* is clear – they would like to spend as much time with their family as possible. In this case, the cohesive unit of partners and children may be at the heart of the *raison d'être*, and the individual action should be to avoid distractions from this time spent with family. What does an outside influence, situation, or event matter if your main goal in life is to spend your time with the people you most love. I doubt anyone sits on their deathbed and says *I forgot to call the cable company to put the account on autopay.* This is obviously a comedic example, but this type of thinking is the same for any small distraction or emergency. In this situation, distractions do not matter.

We have heard of work environments that are so-called *toxic* or *harmful*, and in these cases, especially when trying to advance your own career, it is important to think individualistically with your time, efforts, and associations. It is not worth the risk of headache or heartache by staying in this environment, but if few other good options exist, it is worth protecting oneself in these situations. Self-preservation is more than just making contemporaneous notes for posterity or navigating the mine field of office politics – it is about protecting oneself from the day-to-day stresses, as well as avoiding being caught in the middle of a sticky or dirty situation. Rise above the toxicity and remain above board in everything that you do.

One example of individualism in history is the story of American inventor and businessman Thomas Edison, born in 1847. From a young age, Edison had a fascination with science and invention. He was particularly interested in the technology of the day, including telegraphs and trains, and he spent much of his youth experimenting and tinkering with these devices. As a young man, Edison moved to New York City where he began working as a telegraph operator. He quickly became known for his technical expertise and his ability to fix and improve upon the equipment he worked with. He also began experimenting with electricity and conducting his own scientific research.

In 1869, Edison invented the Universal Stock Printer, which was a machine that could automatically transcribe telegraph messages onto paper. This invention was a major success and earned Edison enough money to start his own laboratory in Menlo Park, New Jersey. At Menlo Park, Edison and his team of assistants worked tirelessly on a wide range of inventions and scientific experiments. Edison's most famous invention, the incandescent light bulb, was developed at Menlo Park and it was patented in 1879. This invention revolutionized the way people lived and worked, as it made it possible to have electric light in homes and businesses.

Edison's invention of the light bulb was just the beginning of his long list of contributions to the field of technology. He also developed the phonograph, which was the first machine to be able to record and play back sound, and the motion picture camera, which was an important development in the history of film. In addition to these inventions, Edison also made important contributions to the field of electrical power generation and transmission, and he was instrumental in the development of the electric power industry.

Throughout his career, Edison was known for his tireless work ethic and his fierce determination to succeed. He worked long hours in his laboratory and was often described as being driven by a fierce passion for invention and discovery. He was also known for his willingness to take risks and his ability to learn from his failures. Although he worked with others on his inventions, it is his fierce individualism by which we can best define him. He was the face of his company, and he stayed in the limelight to help promote his products. In this way, he could be considered a forerunner to Steve Jobs of Apple or Elon Musk of Tesla and SpaceX.

Another example of individualism from history is the story of Marie Curie. Curie was a Polish-born scientist who made groundbreaking contributions to the fields of physics and chemistry in the late 19th and early 20th centuries. she was the first woman to win a Nobel Prize, and the first person to win the award twice. She was also the first female professor at the University of Paris, and the first woman to be awarded a doctorate by the University.

Despite facing discrimination and barriers because of her gender, Curie persisted in her pursuit of scientific knowledge. She independently financed her research and spent long hours working in her lab. Her discoveries, including the discovery of the elements polonium and radium, were a result of her relentless curiosity and passion for science. Her determination and individualism were a source of inspiration for many women in science, and her legacy continues to inspire individuals to this day.

Just as with all other Warrior traits, individualism is a muscle that can be grown with practice. The simplest way to start practicing being individualistic with your time and efforts is to begin saying *no* to people's requests of you, especially when it is not your responsibility to help or otherwise be involved. It is easy to say *yes* to a friend who asks you for help with moving on a weekend. Afterall, you are not working that day, your friend will buy you lunch, and they have helped you as well. It seems like a reasonable request, but if it takes away from your plan or goal, then it is worth saying no. Your friend should already be aware of your large undertaking, but if not, remind them that your time is precious and that you must focus your energies on a goal. It is not always this simple, hence why I mention that the friend has helped you in the past. Our instincts tell us to return the favor, but in lieu of helping, perhaps you can offer to treat the moving crew to lunch or offer to hire and pay for a moving person to help in your place. This may be worth doing even if you simply decide to rest on the weekend. Rest is important, as it can help you see your path with a fresh outlook.

Saying *no* to others' requests is the easiest way to practice individualism but be aware of how you are responding to others – be empathetic. Keep in mind that not everyone is used to saying *no* to a friend, and many friends are not used to hearing *no* from a close friend. Make sure there is a balance – you do not always have to say no if you are practicing, because the person asking you for your time or efforts may take it badly, and this could obviously fray relationships. But when you are engaged with your goal or main activity for which you have worked to become a Warrior, be sure that you make those who are close to you (but outside of your Individual Unit) know about your goals. Chances are they will not ask you for your time or energy during this period. And if they do, they will do so with the understanding that they are asking for a large favor. Helping a friend move? Perhaps. Helping a friend move during your final exams or during a busy time for your business? Definitely not.

Here are some more strategies for improving your individualism.

Set specific, measurable goals for yourself. This will give you a clear sense of direction and purpose, and help you focus on achieving your own unique aspirations. Those in business management know this well: you cannot test what you do not measure. Where should you be in one week or in one month? What kinds of things should you do and in what order? These are questions to ask yourself when setting goals.

Take responsibility for your own actions and decisions. Don't rely on others to guide or validate your choices; instead, trust yourself and your own judgment. This goes back to Thomas Edison: do you think Edison would have been successful had he not trusted himself and his own judgement? Whenever you are embarking on new ventures, there will always be people who say *no* to you. *Everything that is possible has been done already*. Do you think we would have the iPhone if everyone thought this way? Take responsibility and trust yourself.

Cultivate a sense of self-awareness. Pay attention to your thoughts, feelings, and behaviors, and try to understand the underlying motivations and drivers that shape them. We talk about this more in depth in other areas of the book, but it is important to consider your thoughts, feelings, and behaviors when you interact with others. Remember, their experiences and your experiences are different. Do not fall for the trap of listening to advice on a particular topic with which the advisor has no experience. Listen to others who have succeeded in areas you want to succeed, but most of all, listen to your own thoughts, the ultimate arbiter of truth.

Practice self-care. Take care of your physical, emotional, and mental well-being, and make sure that you are getting enough rest, exercise, and healthy food. This is where your Individual Unit may play a role. Remember your *raison d'être* and always keep that front and center. Without your own well-being, you cannot undertake any of the challenges you wish to or meet the goals you would like to achieve.

Surround yourself with people who support and encourage your individuality. Spend time with people who are open-minded, non-judgmental, and genuinely interested in your unique perspective. Remember to reach beyond your regular group of people and expand your horizons. If you are trying to do something that has yet to be done, you need new ideas and new ways of thinking. The people already in your life may not hold all the answers, so it is important to be open to new relationships with people who can help encourage new thoughts.

Lastly, try to focus on your strengths and interests, and take steps to develop them as much as possible. It is many times easier to focus on and grow a skill you already have than learning a new skill from the beginning. Remember we mentioned that some psychologists believe in can take 10,000 hours or more to learn a new skill? Perhaps for a skill you already have, and you are trying to strengthen, the total time of improvement may only be 10 hours. Any time you can recycle a current strength to create a new strength will save you energy and heartache.

Optimism

Optimism is the ability to look to the future with a positive outlook at most matters in our lives. This is different from positivity, which is the attempt to always have and display a positive attitude. Even in the direst of situations we can still be optimistic, which when we are seriously down on our luck in may not always be possible to stay positive. You can be optimistic that things will turn out alright, even when it appears things will not. While positivity and staying positive are moods, optimism is a state of mind. This means it is possible to be optimistic, even when you are feeling down in the dumps and being hard on yourself.

So how does optimism manifest itself and lead to a Warrior Mindset? A Warrior always believes they will win, no matter what the consequences. This optimistic energy is put out into the universe, and that same optimism is reflected in everything the Warrior does. Optimism informs the Warrior's attitude: *Today was an awful day. Tomorrow will be better.* Positivity is the simple emotion of joy or happiness — but being an emotion, it is always fleeting. You can feel joy or happiness one moment because of success in one aspect of your life, but then a few hours go by and that feeling goes away, leaving you with the need to refill that gap with more happiness. Optimism, on the other hand, is never changing because it is not specific – it does not rely on a momentary high or low to work, simply a desire to see the future positively and with anticipation.

Let me share a story about myself that you may find useful regarding optimism. Many people do not know this about me, but I am an amateur pinball player and I play in several amateur leagues and participate in tournaments. I should begin by saying that I am not that good, nor am I too bad. I often tell people *I am somewhere in the middle.* This is true and can be verified by my tournament results – I tend to finish tournaments being ranked somewhere in the middle. I practice and practice, spending hours improving my shots and my overall technique. When I would play tournaments, I used to look at the names of players who signed up and I would often cringe, knowing that these were the best players and that I was sure to lose my match against them. I was constantly pessimistic and filled with negativity – when I saw those names, I became hopeless. I was not thinking about how these players were human and therefore beatable, but to me seeing those names on the roster meant an instant loss. Sure enough, at each tournament I would only prove myself right. During each tournament, I would quickly fill with anxiety and become stressed, then I would lose badly.

  One night, at a regional tournament, I decided I would change my way of thinking. I knew that the top players were beatable, and the only difference between them and me was the confidence to face a tough player and win. I was still filled with negative thoughts about how bad I was as a player, but I decided he would be optimistic. I would play my best, and I would see the other players, not as gods, but as peers. My first tournament with optimism did not go so well. I was still nervous, and I was out in the early rounds. I maintained my optimism and thought that future tournaments would be better. I kept playing with optimism, and after a month I started seeing results. I began finishing tournaments in the top third of players, and soon in the top quarter. One night I was so confident from my optimism that I beat three top players in a row, and I reached the final round – where I lost. Still, I would not be discouraged. I celebrated the win, but was not overly glib about it. I was proud of myself and where I had finished. I kept working hard until he would win a tournament, which would not happen for a long while.

It was my optimism that kept me going and to endure loss after loss. I knew that it was just a matter of time before I would reach my goal, and even if I did not, I kept believing in myself. It all had to do with my optimistic attitude, not becoming complacent when I was improving, and continuing to work toward my goal when it was within striking distance.

Understand that optimism, just like many things in life, is a choice. I made a choice to be optimistic about my tournament results. Optimism is not something you can earn, practice, or wait until it arrives on its own. Optimism is a choice. It is the choice to keep looking on the bright side when life looks dark. It is the choice to not become so happy or sad at a given situation, but to maintain an even keel to keep your emotions in check. One must choose to be optimistic, just as one chooses to be happy or sad.

While optimism is where Warriors choose their own emotional destiny, the sad part is that many who reject the Warrior Mindset instead opt for victimhood through ongoing pessimism. They believe that bad things happen to them because of some reason or another, and do not place any fault on their own negative emotions. Instead of choosing optimism and letting the bad parts of life simply slide off their backs, they decide to focus on negativity and see life as a series of insurmountable challenges. They feel that these things happened to them through no fault of their own and choose pessimism. While things do happen to us in life, even through no fault of our own – our car breaks down, we become ill, or we lose money in an investment – choosing how to look at life, either pessimistically or optimistically, is what will determine our overall happiness and satisfaction with life.

Conclusion

Developing a Warrior Mindset is no small undertaking. It requires immense mental strength and a strong dedication to being proactive in one's own life. Outcomes are not predetermined, but rather depend on the effort expended to make it happen. As the saying goes, *you only get out what you put in.*

In this book we have explored the many qualities of a Warrior, of someone who can approach a situation and attack it as ancient Warriors attacked enemies. With ruthlessness, with learned intelligence, with an attitude that says *never give up*. We have learned stories of regular as well as extraordinary people and learned the lessons they could teach us. At the same time, we have learned that deciding on your *raison d'être* is an incredible motivator for your Journey. The reason we choose to undertake a challenge is as important as the effort we put into the challenge itself. Without motivation, determination, will power, and other abstract ideas about power, we will have a difficult time achieving our goals.

We also learned that intentionality alone is not enough to succeed in most scenarios. We can control our own actions, emotions, thoughts, and decisions, but we cannot control those of others around us. When battling an internal challenge, this is typically not an issue, but when we are challenging a force outside of ourselves, we cannot control the actions or thoughts of another person or persons. Thus, we must be ready to battle with external forces that may place an outcome on our goals. A person battling cancer, for example, can control their own Mindset, the actions of their doctors, and the therapies they decide to undertake, but they cannot predict the direction or progression of their illness, at least not directly.

The qualities of a Warrior

Throughout this book we learned the many qualities of a Warrior and anecdotes describing situations in which each quality was used to a useful degree. When we consider the many qualities of a Warrior, we will notice that many of them are actually very similar, and that's because the Warrior Mindset is about one thing that encompasses all of these qualities: grit. Grit is the overall ability to stick with something for the long term. Grit requires all the traits that make up a Warrior, with passion for your *raison d'être* at the center. Let us quickly re-examine eat quality of a Warrior and understand how each fit with the idea of grit.

Creativity – A Warrior must be creative when existing solutions and outcomes are not useful or do not work I the present situation. There is always a third option. *When there is a will there is a way*, as the saying goes. When you become stuck in a situation, the creativity aspect of grit will push you to be more creative. Do not forget, there is a lot on the line!

Courage – A Warrior must face fear head on by using courage to overcome an obstacle. Courage cannot exist when fear is not present. You are afraid you might fail, you might die, you might lose everything. Push forward, use courage, as informed by your *raison d'être*, to reach for your desired outcome.

Persistence – When a Warrior is told *no,* they must return to the battle at the next opportunity and not give in to the idea of losing. You must believe in your heart that you cannot lose. A loss then becomes a minor setback. Push forward, try again, remember your *raison d'être*.

Resilience – A Warrior must not only come back when defeated, but they must do so with an attitude that tells the world, *I will never give up*. Each time you fail is simply an opportunity to learn. Take your lesson learned, push forward, and try again. There is a lot on the line to not come back stronger.

Determination – A Warrior must have the will power to push through a situation, even at great peril and loss. Determination and motivation are tightly connected, and a Warrior must have determination about a situation to be motivated to challenge it. Are you motivated enough to live, succeed, graduate? You must make the choice to do whatever is necessary. Push forward with every bit of power in your soul.

Adaptability – Situations change from moment to moment, and a Warrior must adapt or risk failure. Nothing in life is certain but change, and adaptability is the key to successfully navigating change. Expect change. Foresee change. Change is inevitable and adapting to a new situation is an incredibly important skill. Adapt or die. Push forward and never forget your *raison d'être*.

Focus – A Warrior must be focused on the issue at hand. Distraction leads to lost energy and effort and switching costs between tasks are too expensive for even a Warrior to handle. Focus and push forward through that focus. Do not allow yourself to become distracted by tiny slivers of gold when the mountaintop holds mounds of it.

Awareness – A Warrior must have an awareness, of themselves, of the situation, of their enemy or challenge. They must learn all they could to overcome their challenge. Being self-aware is a good start – what are your own weaknesses? But knowing your enemy's weaknesses is more important – what are their weaknesses, and how can you push through to overcome them?

Discipline – A Warrior must be disciplined, ready to make sacrifices for the greater goal. Warriors use routines to streamline their time and effort to lose the least amount of energy. Whether it is a routine involving study, diet, exercise, sleep, or lifestyle, you must be disciplined to push through the barriers that stand in your way. You have too much on the line to drop your routine.

Individualism – A somewhat contradictory quality for Warriors to possess, filled with negative connotations, but individualism ensures that Warriors say *yes* to the right things and people, and say *no* to anything that takes away from the primary goal. Your most precious resource is your time – it is finite, there is no way of storing it, and there is no way of getting it back if it is lost. Treat your time as more precious than gold. Say *no* to efforts that take away your time and are unessential. How do you know what is right and what is wrong for you? What does your heart tell you?

Optimism – While happiness, joy, sadness, and anger are emotions, optimism is a choice that we must make. Choose to look for opportunities and to face the day with anticipation. Emotions are short lived, ups and downs created by individual events, but optimism is long lasting because it does not depend on one or two things going right or wrong. Choose to be optimistic.

    These many qualities combined constitute the Warrior Mindset, which can be used to overcome many challenges that are external (outside of oneself) in nature, and all challenges that are internal (inside one's own mind) in nature. With these many qualities, a Warrior can overcome a temporary illness, the loss of a loved one, reach the next level at work, succeed at the highest academic levels, improve their overall station in life, and much more.

www.ingramcontent.com/pod-product-compliance
Lightning Source LLC
Chambersburg PA
CBHW051548010526
44118CB00022B/2625